Praise for

Moments with Malachi

"I'm not a reader, but I don't regret taking the time to read this book. Powell's conversational style had me feeling he was sitting with me talking as I read. It's called *Moments with Malachi* but really you'll spend moments with Powell, Malachi, and Christ, and you'll be able to spend moments with the ones you love strengthened by this book."

> **Topher Rogers**, Real Estate Broker based out of Austin, Texas

"This devotional guides the reader wonderfully through one of the Old Testament's treasures, Malachi. As you read, ancient words will rise up to help meet the challenges of the modern world, and bring you into a deeper relationship with God, our Father and Creator."

> **Aaron Bequette**, Pastor of Northside Christian Center in Carthage, Texas

"The reflections of this devotional come in bite-size "moments" that can be taken daily like spiritual vitamins. The writing is clean and insightful. These solid nuggets of truth will help anyone willing to read this book."

> **Jim Walters**, Senior Pastor, Bear Valley Church, Denver, Colorado

"I had always been curious about how to exactly understand the Old Testament and apply it to my faith. This book has done wonders helping me see my Savior in a new way."

Susan Sowards, Public school teacher at Chireno ISD

"This book is great for personal study or in small groups. Its depth is life changing, but it is still an easy read. *Moments with Malachi* beautifully reveals what a loving God has for those He calls His children. It is amazing to see Jesus on every page of this Old Testament minor prophet.

Matt Sosebee, Dallas area student pastor

"*Moments with Malachi* significantly enhanced my life-group's understanding of the message from Malachi to believers. It was through reading this book that our life-group, including me as the facilitator, made life-changing covenants of obedience to God as our worship to Him."

Steve Prestridge, Student/Worship Pastor at Northside Church, Mineola, TX

Dedicated to The Covenant Community

You give and take away (I SAID YA) *give and take away.*

Up and Out Publishing
Moments with Malachi: New Testament Insights
from the Old Testament's Last Book
Michael Powell

Editors: Jean Brannon, Mandy Powell, Tammy Fish
Cover Design: Jessica Rainey
Interior Design and Layout: Tim Tyler

Published in the United States by Up and Out Publishing
ISBN. 9781522938309

Version 1.1
Printed by CreateSpace, a DBA of On-Demand Publishing,
LLC

www.upandoutpublishing.com

Moments with Malachi
New Testament Insights from the Old
Testament's Last Prophet
By Michael Powell

Up and Out Publishing
Buncombe, Texas
www.upandoutpublishing.com

Contents

Foreword

Even after Bible College, I had never really looked into the pages of this small book of prophecy at the end of the Old Testament. I thought the book of Malachi was meant to tell me I was almost to the New Testament. Little did I know this book was full of insights and truths about the heart of God and who He desires His people to be. As I began reading *Moments with Malachi*, I realized that the people of Malachi's time were so very much like the church.

After reading the book twice (I'm a bit slow), I began thinking of God more correctly.

I began to see a better picture of what grace is. And I began to see myself more humbly.

Being a Youth Pastor, I did what all the greats do, I used this material to teach in my youth ministry. When I announced to my youth leaders that we were going to go on a journey through the Book of Malachi, they thought that I was crazy. I gave them each a book and they began to see the deep truths of God that I had discovered.

My students benefited from the words on these pages. As we embarked on a journey to read through Malachi and to look at the book, *Moments with Malachi*, I began to see my students grow in deeper ways. The discussions were deep and intense, and I saw students have those *aha* moments that youth ministers dream of. They got excited about a book that was changing their life and growing their theology!

My friend, Michael Powell, has an amazing heart for his God. He does a tremendous job of making a book written 400 B.C. so very relevant to us today. From relationships with God, our parents, our children, and our marriages, to theology, blessings, and covenants, this book's message for us is easy to read and understand.

I encourage you to read *Moments with Malachi* with an open heart, expecting truths to change who you are so that your heart would not be like the people of Malachi's day.

~ Matt Sosebee

Introduction

One of the greatest worship services my church ever experienced was at a wedding. Many of us drove over three hours to celebrate the union of Chris and Cassidy. I can't think of a time when I have been so proud to be a pastor.

The event symbolized well the nature of our church. We celebrated romance during the wedding. We celebrated community at the reception. We celebrated dependency afterwards as five cars caravanned back at three in the morning. We celebrated Christ all along the way.

Malachi would have enjoyed the event. His book pleads for genuine romance to   replace neglect and adultery. He begs for community during horrible struggles for power. He invites dependence upon the LORD, but is rejected and scorned.

The message of Malachi is easy to read and understand. Just do the opposite of what those who first heard the words of Malachi were doing. Malachi is a prophetic book written not because the people were failing to worship or offer sacrifices, but because the people weren't interested in God anymore.

Those Malachi addressed were not great active sinners; they were great passive sinners. They weren't running towards evil. They just weren't running towards righteousness and God. They were minimalists asking, "What does God require?" and then making sure they didn't do one thing more than what the letter of the law said to do.

Written around 400 BC, the temple and city wall had been rebuilt, but the Jews had failed to rebuild their own souls. They weren't interested in God. The heartbeat of Malachi and the purpose of this devotional are to stimulate your interest in God. You may be interested enough to begin reading this book, but Malachi will soon show that often our standard of interest may fall far short of God's. May God draw you nearer to His standard and closer to His heart as you read!

CHAPTER ONE

A joyous burden

"The burden of the word of the Lord to Israel by Malachi…" Malachi 1:1

Today we will simply look at the title of the book; the first verse. "The burden of the word of the Lord to Israel by Malachi." When Malachi finished his ministry, it came time to place a heading over his message. Interestingly, he chose to call it a burden.

I assume it was a joyous burden. In other words, if Malachi had to do it again, knowing the burden beforehand, he would still do it. But nevertheless, he didn't hide the fact that obeying God was burdensome.

Other prophets hint at this without being as blunt as Malachi. Isaiah asked, "Who has believed our report?" which could also be translated, "Who has taken us seriously?" Jeremiah fell into such a depression he cried, "Woe is me, my mother, that you have borne me." Elijah complained he wasn't as good as the prophets before him, and Moses looked to God more than once and said, "Just kill me!"

None of these cries came because of persecution these men faced. They are the cries of emotional and spiritual strain that comes from carrying God's Word. This is the joyous burden God invites you to endure. Knowing this burden, will you carry His Word?

Carrying His Word is a burden because it is always heavy, and because it is often rejected. There are very few fluffy passages in the Bible. Instead there are hard passages like the one we'll have to examine tomorrow, "Jacob the Lord has loved, but Esau He has hated."

The weight of glory is often more than we can bear. It is a joyous burden to have to carry Romans 8:28, "We know that all things work together for good to those who love God, to those who are the called according to His purpose," when thousands are dying of natural disasters, poverty, and malnutrition.

It is a joyous burden to carry 1st John 4:8, "God is love," when our parents are clinically depressed or sent off to war, or using drugs, or disapproving of our spouse, or worse – have passed away.

It is a joyous burden to have to carry Psalm 146:9, "The Lord relieves the orphan," when in Africa there are 13 million AIDS-related orphans.

The Word is too good for us. It is too heavy for us. The only faithful option we have is to allow the Word to carry us instead of vice versa. We are people with dim spiritual eyes. Bright light painfully stretches the pupil of our soul.

The word of God is also heavy because it is rejected. If we carry the Word of the Lord to people as Malachi did, we will be rejected. We will be called arrogant and intolerant. We will be called judgmental.

I once went with someone to witness in a laundry mat. During our prayer time beforehand he told the few of us, "Don't worry if you get rejected. Just remember they are rejecting God, not you." All of us nodded our heads, but then I considered the statement.

"Don't worry, they're rejecting God..." That's exactly what I was worried about! Who cares if they reject me; I have no power over their eternal residence. The Word of God grew heavier and heavier in me as I realized, "They aren't rejecting me; they are rejecting the only begotten Son of God." The punishment for this crime is eternal damnation.

It is a joyous burden to bring water to a man dying of thirst knowing he may very well throw the water back in your face and die in front of you. It is horrible to offer someone a parachute and watch them collapse to the earth beneath. It is a joyous burden to know that you possess the antidote to a condition more deadly than cancer, AIDS, and terrorism. You have within you the means to conquer death, but still many people will die.

When Malachi spoke his message, it was a burden because the words were heavy and the congregation was sinful. It is still a burden to carry God's truth because the words are heavy and some who hear won't take them and increase the joy of their life. Carrying the Word of God weighs heavily upon you.

So why do it? Why listen to Jesus say, "Take up your cross and follow Me?" There is one great answer – because it's worth it. As long as God has interacted with man, no man has regretted following God. The cost is nothing compared to the reward.

We must live our lives in a way that would appear totally wasteful if there were no God and heaven. We can live our lives this way because we "consider the sufferings of this present time are not worthy to be compared with the glory that shall be revealed in us." We must live our lives in such a way that upon our dying breath we might pronounce it a burden, but after that breath, a joyous burden totally worth it.

Spending moments with Malachi will place you on the narrow road. It is a road that is harder than the broad way. It is steep and rocky and winds back and forth – there are very few who find it. But Jesus says its way leads to life. The joyous burden soon enough will become only joy. We will reach the top of the narrow path to find a view of glory we could have never imagined, and our smiling Savior saying, "Well done, My good and faithful servant."

Discussion Questions and Journal Space

1. How do you live within the tension of joy and pain as you follow Jesus?

2. When was a time you experienced great sorrow and great joy at once?

3. What encouragement do you think God gave to Malachi through His Spirit as Malachi ministered to rebellious religious people?

_____

_____

_____

_____

_____

_____

_____

CHAPTER TWO

How has God loved us?

If you are interested in God you will move
towards Him, you will explore Him,
and you will tell others about Him.

We've considered the title of Malachi given in
verse one, "The burden of the word of the Lord
to Israel by Malachi." Now a burden is handed to
us as we consider some of the heaviest words in
the Bible.

*"I have loved you,' says the LORD, "Yet you say, 'In
what way have You loved us?' 'Was not Esau
Jacob's brother?' says the LORD, 'Yet Jacob I have
loved, but Esau I have hated.'"* – Malachi 1:2-3a

Why in the world would God hate Esau? It doesn't seem fair for God to hate anyone. You may have a hard time believing God is even capable of hating. Most people share these sentiments. But we all have a problem with the wrong quote. We shouldn't be surprised that He hated Esau. We should marvel that He loved Jacob.

If God is holy we should not be bothered with His judgment as much as His grace. If God is holy we should be more disturbed that people are getting into heaven than that people are going to hell. It should startle us that God would extend forgiveness. It shouldn't surprise us as much when He extends His wrath. People have insulted the worth of God and deserve to be punished with torture. It should blow our minds that God rescues some from this.

Consider the exodus. God parts the Red Sea and allows the Israelites to pass through safely on dry land. When the Egyptians try the same, God throws down the water and they die the horrible death. As the Jews look into the water they can hear the words of God, "I have loved you, but Egypt I have hated."

What's the appropriate response in that moment? Are the Israelites supposed to be bothered with the fact that thousands of Egyptians just drowned? Those sentiments may have come as the bodies washed onto the shore, but their overwhelming emotion was joy. Exodus 14:30 – 15:2 describes their reaction.

"So the LORD saved Israel that day out of the hand of the Egyptians and Israel saw the Egyptians dead on the seashore. Thus Israel saw the great work which the LORD had done in Egypt; so the people feared the LORD, and believed the LORD and His servant Moses. Then Moses and the children of Israel sang this song to the LORD, and spoke saying, 'I will sing to the LORD for He has triumphed gloriously! The horse and the rider He has thrown into the sea. The LORD is my strength and song, And He has become my salvation; He is my God, and I will praise Him..."

It is very dangerous to think God owes you something. It would have been a horrible sin for the Jews to witness the choice of God to rescue them and destroy the Egyptians and think, "Why did God allow them to drown?" God could allow them to drown because He didn't owe them anything.

Likewise, it would have been a horrible sin for the Jews to witness the choice of God to rescue them and destroy the Egyptians and think, "Well of course God didn't drown us!" He could have allowed them to drown because He didn't owe them anything either.

When you understand that God doesn't owe you anything, and you get something from God, you're able to worship with surprise. When bad and good happen around you at the same time, and you happen to receive the good – tremble. Tremble as you look at the bodies washing ashore, and then sing to the God who has left you standing.

Also, when you understand God doesn't owe you anything, and then you have the waves of misery crash down upon you, you're able to pray with patience instead of bitterness. When bad and good happen around you at the same time and you happen to receive the bad – tremble. Tremble as you consider you deserve far worse punishment for sin.

The Jews Malachi addresses did not have an obedient reaction to God's grace. They were not surprised that God had delivered them out of the hand of Assyria and allowed them to return to Jerusalem to rebuild the temple and the city wall. They were not surprised that God offered forgiveness to them for their sins. They had forgotten an important truth; God owns all and owes none.

In this moment with Malachi we must stop taking grace for granted. We must never carry an attitude of deserving all we gain. When God says, "I have loved you," we must never question in return, "How have you loved us?"

Instead let the question mark be conquered by a point of exclamation. Let this question become our song, "How have you loved us!"

Discussion Questions and Journal Space

1. Why do you think blessings that surprise us at first become taken for granted in time? What can you do in your own life to limit this sin?

2. What would your emotions have been, do you think, if you were an Israeli watching Egyptians wash up on the shore?

3. Does God's absolute authority and freedom increase your love for Him or tempt you to pull away from Him?

_____

_____

_____

_____

_____

_____

_____

_____

_____

_____

_____

_____

_____

_____

_____

_____

_____

_____

_____

_____

_____

CHAPTER THREE

God loves us as He loved Jacob

Certainly the heart of God is pained when we challenge His love rather than celebrate it.

I have a son named Miles, and to imagine him one day returning my "I love you" with "Yeah right, how have you loved me?" puts pain in my chest and stomach.

Perhaps I would answer Miles with a paraphrase of God's words found in Malachi. That answer would go something like this, "Consider the other kids who live on this street, Miles. I am not interested in their heritage. When I die I will leave nothing to them. Even if they behave better than you, they get nothing from me. I do not invite them to live in my house or eat at my table. There is nothing they could do to cause me to choose them above you. If I had to choose for all of them to die so you could live I'd do it without thinking twice or having any guilt. Would you like to have a look outside and pick another house to live? You best remember, I brought you into this world, and I can take you out."

God is not required to love us. All love we receive should stimulate worship. God owes us no details concerning why or how He loves us. Still, He answers the question. Let's spend a moment with Malachi examining the answer of God in Malachi 1:2-3.

"'Was not Esau Jacob's brother?' says the LORD. Yet Jacob I have loved, but Esau I have hated. And laid waste his mountains and his heritage for the jackals of the wilderness."

Even though the people of Malachi questioned God's love by asking, "In what way have You loved us?" God was good enough to answer them. There is a particular way God loved them, and it is the same way God loves us. God loves us the way He loved Jacob. There are three primary ways God loved Jacob: before birth, in spite of sin, and without comparison.

Before Jacob was born God told his mother that he would be preferred over his brother. Genesis 25:23 says, "Two nations are in your womb, two peoples shall be separated from your body; one people shall be stronger than the other, and the older shall serve the younger."

God loved you before you were born as well. You are able to say like David, "You knit me together in my mother's womb. I am fearfully and wonderfully made." And God says to you like He did to Jeremiah, "Before I formed you in the womb I knew you; before you were born I sanctified you."

Paul was writing heavy but true words in Romans 8:29-30. "Whom He foreknew, He also predestined to be conformed to the image of His Son, that He might be the firstborn among many brethren. Moreover whom He predestined, these He also called; whom He called, these He also justified; and whom He justified; these he also glorified."

God loved you before you were born. He was not surprised the day you embraced Christ because He always knew you would gain entrance into heaven and spend eternity with Him. He loved you before you were born – just like He did Jacob.

The second way God loved Jacob was in spite of sin. Jacob was a great sinner. He lied to his old, blind father, pretending to be Esau so he could gain the blessings of the firstborn. He ran away from home out of fear that his brother would kill him with another lie, "God wants me to go find a bride."

When he found a bride he worked a scheme to steal his father-in-law's livestock. He had no sort of prayer life until years later when he heard Esau was coming to meet him and he feared for his life. His very name means, "Deceiver, Liar." This is who God loves?

If we are going to fully enjoy God's grace we should admit daily that we are no better than Jacob. We have all fallen short of the standard of God's glory. His standard is perfection, and we don't have perfect lives. We don't have perfect days. We don't have perfect hours. We don't have perfect minutes.

We should ask not, "What sin is there in me?" but, "What sin is there not in me?" God loves us in spite of our sin. While we were still sinners Christ died for us. God loves you - knowing your past sins, your present sins, and your future sins!

God loves you by taking your sins and casting them as far as the east is from the west. As certain as Jesus died and came back to life, your sins are erased and your heart is full of righteousness. In spite of your sin, Jesus died for you, and in spite of your sin, Jesus called your name, and in spite of your sin, you answered Him.

"For I call My sheep by name and they recognize My voice and follow Me," said Jesus. Notice, we are not made God's sheep because we recognize His voice – we recognize His voice because we are already His sheep. Before we were born we were destined to become His sheep and our sin could not disqualify us because Jesus died so our sin could be erased.

Finally, God loved Jacob without comparison. In other words, He loved him freely. God didn't choose Jacob as the lesser of two evils. He picked him without manipulation, completely freely. God loved Jacob so we would celebrate God's grace, not Jacob's worth. It is God who is great and impressive, not Jacob. Jacob has no room for boasting.

One day we will all be gathered before the throne of God, and He will separate every individual who has ever lived into two groups. The sheep will be on His right and the goats on His left. In that moment you may examine your life and suddenly think, "How has He loved me? I've fooled myself. This brilliantly shining, radiant Being has seen all of my sins! He hates evil, and I am full of what He hates. There were a thousand goods I could have done, but refused to do. There were a thousand evils I could have avoided, but I refused to avoid. He hasn't loved me. I am going to be eternally tortured."

Then Jesus will say with a stern, bass drum voice, "Depart from Me, I never knew you." You may imagine a trap door opening and your body falling into hell. But Jesus lifts your chin up, and says with eyes full of love, "Well done, My good and faithful servant. Enter into the joy prepared for you from the foundations of the world."

In that moment we won't think, "Shouldn't God give everyone entrance into heaven?" We won't think, "Well of course He is letting me in." Instead, we'll see clearly that God loves freely whomever He wishes to love, and only eternity is long enough to say thanks.

Discussion Questions and Journal Space

1. How would your life change if you truly believed that God loved you in spite of your sin?

2. Some people think that if you know God's love doesn't fluctuate according to your behavior you'll sin more. Do you agree?

_____

_____

_____

_____

_____

CHAPTER FOUR

Giving our Dad His due

God is required to love no one.
God loves us.

God loves us to the utmost. There is nothing you could do to get God to love you anymore than He does now. You have the daily opportunity to gain maximum love from the King of the universe! The love of God pours like Niagara Falls upon all who belong to Christ.

Those are the facts about God's interaction towards us. Today, as you spend a moment with Malachi, focus upon the appropriate reaction to these facts. He loves us – now what? Malachi 1:6 gives the answer.

"'A son honors his father, and a servant his master. Then if I am a father, where is My honor? And if I

*am a master, where is My respect?' says the Lord
of hosts to you, O priests who despise My name.
But you say, 'How have we despised Your name?'"*

How do you respond to God's amazing grace? You do the opposite of the Jews Malachi preached to – give God your very best. You don't give God your best to manipulate His love. You give God your best to say thank you and to position yourself under the mighty waterfall of grace so you become drenched with the Living Water of Christ.

Today's verse provokes an important question, "Why do we sin?" We should search our hearts for an answer. Why do we sin against a loving, but fierce God who owes us nothing but offers us His only begotten Son? Why do we block God's love?

God shows these sinners the source of their sin when He asks them, "If I am a father, where is my honor? If I am a master, where is my respect?" They have forgotten who God is, and forgetting God leads quickly to sin.

God is our Father. He deserves much respect. Malachi uses a father-child relationship because back in Malachi's day, children actually obeyed and honored their parents.

Being a father means being responsible and respected. As a dad, I am responsible for the livelihood of my family. If they don't eat, it's my fault. That responsibility demands respect. Since God is going to hold me accountable I should demand they follow me not only for their own sake, but for my sake as well.

In Malachi's day people understood this well. The father of the home was to be respected without condition. Leviticus 20:9 stated, "If anyone curses his father or mother, he must be put to death. He has cursed his father or his mother, and his blood will be on his own head."

Deuteronomy 21:18-21 is more graphic.

"If a man has a stubborn and rebellious son who does not obey his father and mother and will not listen to them when they discipline him, his father and mother shall take hold of him and bring him to the elders at the gate of his town. They shall say to the elders, 'This son of ours is stubborn and rebellious. He will not obey us. He is a profligate and a drunkard.' Then all the men of his town shall stone him to death. You must purge the evil from among you. All Israel will hear of it and be afraid."

There is no record in the Bible or in any documented history of the Jews that parents stoned their children. Children feared their parents because they could be killed if they didn't, but it was fear mixed with love and respect because they recognized their parents cared for them and didn't want them getting stoned.

We easily forget what those originally hearing Malachi's words forgot; God has the authority and power to kill us, but the love and grace not to. If the Jews hearing Malachi had remembered this they would have given God the same respect they gave their earthly fathers.

This concept applies to us in an even deeper way. We are not God's children the way Malachi's audience was. We are not Jewish, and we are living after the death and resurrection of Jesus. This means we are adopted into God's family.

Under the laws of those days, adopted children were especially protected. When a father adopted a child, he surrendered the right of stoning. This policy was meant to give the orphan a sense of security. Romans 8:15 explains further, "For you did not receive a spirit that makes you a slave again to fear, but you received the Spirit of adoption. And by him we cry, 'Abba, Father.'"

We have been adopted! God, in His grace, has thrown away the right to kill us. If you are a saved person you can live without insecurity knowing beyond a shadow of a doubt that God will not allow you to be lost. Like a good Father, He is responsible for your eternal   livelihood. Like a good child we should remember this and give Him extreme respect.

Keeping your spouse on your mind may save you from an affair. Being watched by your teachers can keep you from cheating. Remembering   who

God is, and that He always watches us, can do much to stimulate better living.

Why do we sin? We forget who God is. It is hard to sin while meditating on God's grace and holiness and power. This is why each day we must sear upon our hearts and minds, "God exists, and He is our Father!"

Are you practicing His presence with daily prayer? Are you reading His Word every day? Are you fellowshipping with other believers regularly in a meaningful way? Are you taking every opportunity to share the gospel with those lost? Are you serving the least?

We are so sinful it only takes a day to forget God. If you don't have ten minutes set aside every day to acknowledge God as the Ultimate Reality of the universe and the Intimate Redeemer of your soul, you're asking for trouble. May God never have to ask us, "Where is My respect?"

Discussion Questions and Journal Space

1. What are you doing everyday to help keep God on your mind? What more should you be doing?

2. How are the relationships in your immediate family? Do you think these relationships reflect your relationship with God?

3. Who are the people you most respect in this world? Where does God's respect rank among them?

_____

_____

_____

_____

_____

_____

_____

CHAPTER FIVE

Lame sacrifices

We must never forget about God

We start a journey down the broad way of destruction as soon as we forget about God. When God is ignored, it becomes easy to offer lame sacrifices. God is not fooled by activity or ritual. He demands our best all the time in every situation.

"You are presenting defiled food upon My altar. But you say, 'How have we defiled You?' In that you say, 'The table of the Lord is to be despised.' But when you present the blind for sacrifice, is it not evil? And when you present the lame and sick, is it not evil? Why not offer it to your governor? Would he be pleased with you? Or would he receive you kindly?' says the Lord of hosts. But

*now will you not entreat God's favor, that He may
be gracious to us?"* - Malachi 1:7-9

These Jews sinned two ways. They despised the table of the Lord, and they gave sorry sacrifices. The first sin has to do with their heart, and the second with their action. Notice that both sins occurred as the people gave. This means externally all is well. They were attending temple and staying very religious. They had lost their joy, and it is a great sin not to be as happy as you possibly can.

We despise the table of God when we complain about how narrow the path is. When we cry, "Woe is me, for I am a Christian," we are committing the first sin of these Jews. From there it becomes extremely easy to begin sinning in the second way. We must never begin to cut corners or stop bringing our best to God.

That's exactly, however, what these Jews had begun to do. Malachi accuses them of bringing blind and lame animals to sacrifice. God says to them in verse eight, "But when   you present the blind for sacrifice, is it not evil? And when you present the lame and sick, is it not evil? Why not offer it to your governor? Would he be pleased with you? Or would he receive you kindly?" says the LORD of hosts."

Bringing lame and blind sacrifices turns the altar into a dump. Too often we don't bring our best to honor God; we bring our unwanted to get rid of it. These Jews were giving to God what they wouldn't even give their governor.

How might you be doing this? Do you think you are generous simply because you offer what you no longer want? I remember once getting new furniture - which allowed us to give our old furniture away to a newly married couple, Chris and Cassidy (mentioned in the introduction). There is nothing generous about this. There's no sacrifice in giving something that isn't needed.

Think about all the people who give clothes to Goodwill and feel like they've really made a sacrifice. The clothes they give are second-hand. No one would dream of giving all their new Christmas clothes and continuing to wear the same old clothes another year! But that is exactly what God demands. He is not a second-hand God. He is a first-fruit God.

It's hardly an insult to say to a friend, "Hey, I don't want this anymore, do you want it?" because they may indeed need it. It is quite an insult, however, to God because He is not in need of anything. We don't give to God to feed Him; we give to God to feed ourselves.

Jesus applied this idea as He watched people give money in the temple. He said the widow who gave two pennies gave more than the businessmen who had hundreds of dollars? How is that? Could it be that Jesus doesn't measure our gifts by what we give, but rather by what we have left after giving?

Measuring the time and money and talent you have after surrendering it to the Lord tells you whether you've made a sacrifice or not. If I am unemployed, and spend three hours serving a sick friend, it's not nearly as sacrificial as if I work 60 hours a week, but give three hours toward comfort. It's not the amount you give, but the amount from which you give that God evaluates.

How awful would these Jews feel about their sin if they realized their offerings foreshadowed the ultimate offering to come? Jesus, God's spotless Lamb, would be brought to the slaughter table of God. When these Jews brought lame and blind sheep with a heart that despised the activity, they were representing God in an embarrassing way.

Each day, all we do symbolizes the importance of Jesus. When we walk the straight and narrow with reluctance, or when we take short cuts that are out of bounds, we make God look small. To say God is worthy is to say God is worth it. This must be our solid belief and practice.

Let's bring offerings to God that can accurately be called sacrifices. Let's give what we want, even desperately need, rather than what we have little desire to keep. Let's give offerings that announce the magnitude and mercy of God. Let's bring them today.

Discussion Questions and Journal Space

1. How often do you have a negative attitude about the demands of Christian living? How can you battle this?

2. Are you willing to give a costly sacrifice, a possession that's worth something and you would miss? How tightly do you hold your possessions?

3. How do our own sacrifices connect with God's ultimate sacrifice of His own Son?

_____

_____

_____

_____

_____

_____

_____

_____

_____

_____

_____

_____

_____

_____

_____

_____

_____

_____

_____

_____

CHAPTER SIX

Good guardrails

Malachi isn't just sound and fury.
He gives practical insights too.

Malachi gives three strategies to stop sinning. They serve as guardrails along the straight and narrow path. I hope this moment with Malachi will persuade you to grab hold of these and implement them in your life.

"Why not offer it to your governor? Would he be pleased with you? Or would he receive you kindly?' says the Lord of hosts. But now will you not entreat God's favor, that He may be gracious to us? 'Oh that there were one among you who would shut the gates, that you might not uselessly kindle fire on My altar! I am not pleased with you,'

says the LORD of hosts, 'nor will I accept an offering from you.'" Malachi 1:7-10

Here you have what could be called the Malachi ethic. The anthem of this ethic is "You wouldn't offer it to your governor, would you?" We can avoid sin and measure our respect for and interest in God by comparing it with our respect and interest toward other, less important people.

If you go two days without talking to Christ you might hear His conviction, "You wouldn't offer that to your spouse, would you?" If you avoid reading God's Word you might hear, "You wouldn't avoid your favorite magazine, would you?" If you skip corporate worship you might hear God say, "You wouldn't skip out on work that easily, would you?" We shouldn't be comfortable treating God more poorly than we treat humans.

Malachi's ethic is basically this – if a human would be insulted with your effort or your gift, then God is greatly insulted. You may want to begin using the Malachi ethic today.

Sometimes it's easier to have a human as a standard for a while then you can build your way up to following God's standard.

This is why I read Christian biographies. I recently read a biography on Francis of Assisi. Every morning I would read a chapter and then ask God to help me be more like Francis. Of course I long to be like Jesus, but He's so far off from my capabilities that I am aiming a little lower.

I want to be more like John Piper. I want to be more like John Woolman. I want to be more like John Wesley. And if I met any of these Johns, I would not despise them, nor would I offer them leftovers. If I have much respect for the John's I don't know, how much more respect should I have for the Jesus I do?

A second guardrail to place on the straight and narrow is in verse nine. "'But now will you not entreat God's favor, that He may be gracious to us? With such an offering on your part, will He receive any of you kindly?' says   the

LORD of hosts." There is no way we'll stop sinning unless we entreat God's favor.

No matter how casual you become in your Christianity there is always hope to gain mercy from God. Think of your sins, not the fact that you're a sinner, but a specific sin you commit on a regular basis. What is something you do that you must stop doing? What is something you aren't doing that you must start doing? What is something you do with a complaining heart? Now, hold that before God in your mind and ask Him to exchange that sin for His grace.

He is faithful and just to forgive us our sins and cleanse us of past unrighteousness. He will give good things to those who ask Him. He is merciful to us and remembers we are but dust. He is willing to cast our sins as far as the east is from the west. He looks at you with love and says, "Go and sin no more." We must entreat God for mercy to stop sinning. We must hate our sin because it acts as a dam that blocks the waterfall of God's love.

Finally, Malachi encourages us to make public our hidden sin. In verse ten God exclaims, "Oh that there were one among you who would shut the gates, that you might not uselessly kindle fire on My altar! I am not pleased with you," says the LORD of hosts, "nor will I accept an offering from you." God says, "Stop pretending that everything is okay. When you do that, I wish you would just stop going to the temple at all."

Nothing would be more spiritual than for congregations and individual Christians to stop pretending everything is okay. Confession must be part of the culture of every church. Telling people how you have been just going through the motions will help stop those same motions, and spark new obedience.

We don't confess to be judged. We confess so we can live honest lives. Someone admitting sin is far more righteous than someone who hides it and pretends all is well. I dare you to try confession. Share with someone a hidden sin. Chances are they won't respond with, "You did what?!" but will instead spread the love of God upon you.

The straight and narrow is also steep and slippery. Many have fallen off along the way. Build guardrails in your life so that when you fall, repentance and restoration occur quickly. Respect God more than all others, ask for His mercy, and confess your sins. This will pave the way for a life of worthy sacrifice.

Discussion Questions and Journal Space

1. Most Christians would say they love God more than anyone else. Can you say honestly that you treat God better than anyone?

2. What changes would occur if you began treating the people around you like you treat the God above you?

3. Who is someone you could begin to be more like that would make you more like Jesus in the process?

_____

_____

_____

_____

_____

_____

_____

_____

_____

_____

_____

_____

_____

_____

CHAPTER SEVEN

God will be famous

"'From the rising of the sun, even to its setting, My name shall be great among the nations, and in every place incense is going to be offered to My name, and a grain offering that is pure; for My name will be great among the nations' says the LORD of hosts. 'For I am a great King' says the Lord of hosts, 'And My name is to be feared among the nations.'" – Malachi 1:11, 14

As magnificent as our sins are, God's magnitude casts a shadow over them when we repent. A moment with Malachi today will help us see that this same individual forgiveness is offered globally to stimulate praise from every nation. Our God is a great and global King.

God's ultimate plan is to surround Himself with all sorts. We must never picture heaven   as one color, or one culture, or one language. Every knee shall bow and every language will confess that Jesus Christ is LORD. We will look and see a multitude from every nation, tribe, and tongue saying, "You are worthy for You were slain, and by Your blood You purchased men for God."

From the rising of the sun to the setting of the sun God's name will be praised. That means in every geographical location. Every Sunday is a twenty-four hour, global worship session. It starts in Australia, moves to the Philippines, then China. Next worship begins in India, then Afghanistan, then Russia. Around three in the morning central standard time, churches in Poland begin their praise. Nigeria is next, then Spain.

The Spanish turns to Portugal as Brazil begins and then turns back to Spanish with Venezuelan voices. As believers of Venezuela exit, New York City bows its head and prays. While they lunch in the Bronx, they worship in Chicago, then those in Phoenix celebrate His grace. Those in Seattle come next, and finally Hawaii worships to end the majestic weekly concert.

Any given Sunday, God gains praise every minute from some congregation or at least some individual, and still, He is not gaining nearly enough praise. If every day were Sunday, He would still not get enough praise. In heaven, after a million trillion years have passed – He will still be worthy of more praise. There will never be a moment when the praised quota gets filled.

God knows this. He declares Himself the great King. Someday Christ is going to split the eastern sky, and in the twinkling of an eye, we will all be changed. An everlasting worship celebration will begin which forever builds in intensity and intimacy. And all the nations will be represented!

Do you imagine heaven correctly? Many imagine a heaven of individual, American bliss. We miss the repetition of heaven's description, namely that God is there in all His splendor, and the nations are there with all of their praise.

Heaven is a mosaic of God's mercy to the nations. Someday we will find ourselves around God's throne, and there with us will be a "great multitude that no one can count, from every nation, tribe, people, and language, standing before the throne and in front of the Lamb."

It is easy for us to do today what Jews did in the day of Malachi. We assume that God respects our national identity. We must admit that Christ is not for one culture over another. The West does not have some special agreement with Christ unavailable to others.

Joshua 5:13-15 teaches as much. "And it came to pass, when Joshua was by Jericho, that he lifted his eyes and looked, and behold, a Man stood opposite him with His sword drawn in His hand. And Joshua went to Him and said, 'Are you for us or for our adversaries?'"

This seems like a timely question, but the response shows us that Joshua's scope of reality was too small. The messenger did not have to be for or against anyone. He answers, "'No, but as Commander of the army of the Lord I have now come.' And Joshua fell on his face to the earth and worshiped."

It was not the Commander that had to choose sides; it was Joshua. So it is today. The question is not whether Christ is for this nation or that ethnic group. The question is, "are you for Christ and for reaching all the ethnic groups?" He is for all peoples and will redeem them for His glory and their eternal enjoyment.

Our God is a great King. He is a global King. We therefore, must begin to represent Him globally. While dealing with our individual sins we must also contribute to the good of the world. God will be famous. We must spread His fanfare.

Discussion Questions and Journal Space

1. How does picturing a multi-ethnic heaven change your view of God or missions or worship?

2. Why is it, do you think, that we are so determined to have God on our side, but not intent to make sure we are on His side?

_____

_____

_____

_____

_____

_____

_____

_____

_____

CHAPTER EIGHT

Turning blessings into curses

Every Christian is a priest.

The role of the priest was to be an intercessor between God and the people. If a priest did His job well, the people would embrace God in a greater way. If a priest did his job poorly, God would be misrepresented and the people would soon fall into sin. The priests of Malachi's day misrepresented God horribly.

"And now, O priests, this commandment is for you. If you will not hear, and if you will not take it to heart, to give glory to My name,' says the Lord of hosts, 'I will send a curse upon you, and I will curse your blessings. Yes, I have cursed them already, because you do not take it to heart. Behold, I will

rebuke your descendants and spread refuse on your faces, the refuse of your solemn feasts; and one will take you away with it. Then you shall know that I have sent this commandment to you, that My covenant with Levi may continue...But you have departed from the way; you have caused many to stumble at the law. You have corrupted the covenant of Levi." – Malachi 2:1-4, 8

Today followers of God do not meet in a temple. There is no need to bring sacrificial lambs with you to worship. The Old Testament priesthood has passed. All animal sacrifices were shadows pointing towards the ultimate sacrifice, Christ. Upon the cross, He offered the perfect sacrifice making null and void any others.

Still, there are priests within the church. The role of offering sacrifices has stopped; however, the goal of bringing people to God continues. Every Christian is now a priest, and the church is a priesthood. Even more solemn than the task of sacrifice, we have the task of reincarnating Christ's death, burial, and resurrection. He is our great High Priest. We are His priesthood.

As priests, we must be sure we are avoiding the rebuke of Malachi. As we take a moment with Malachi today, we see five accusations thrown against the priests of his day. Exploring them one at a time may help us be found innocent of such crimes.

God, speaking through Malachi, accuses the priests of no longer hearing His voice. Tragedy has struck when believers no longer tune into the frequency of God. Regularly we should listen. We do this by sitting in silence. We do this by reading the Bible. We do this through prayer. We do this through observing nature and people. Whatever avenue, we must continue to hear God. Refusing to hear Him invites His curse and kills our witness.

Another accusation, these priests do not take God's glory to heart. The desire of their souls had ceased to be amplifying God's worth with their lives. May it never be for us. God's glory must be the motivating factor for all our actions. The anthem of John the Baptizer must be our own, "I must decrease, but He must increase." The answer to every "why?" is for God's glory.

These priests had departed from the way. The very first name for the church was "the Way." Jesus called Himself, "the Way, the Truth, and the Life." We have been created to walk a certain path. There is a way for us to live, and we must abide in it. We hear God's voice in our minds. We embrace God's glory in our hearts. We practice God's way in our actions.

In Malachi's day, many looked to the priests as examples of obedient living. When a priest failed morally, it stimulated great moral failure in the entire nation. Likewise, today when a pastor fails, many stumble as a result. We are told that not many should strive to become teachers because there is a stricter judgment for them.

Today, Christians continue to cause many to stumble because of poor moral living. Jesus gave the lost an ability to recognize His children.

He said, "They will know you by your love." If we refuse or neglect to love each other, we are causing many to stumble. Being the salt and light of the world, we are responsible for representing Christ in a way that increases the desire of meeting Him. Too often, the greatest reason people refuse God as their heavenly Father is because they don't want Christians as their spiritual brothers and sisters.

All of these failures connect. When we refuse to hear God's voice we will soon care less for His glory. If we are cold concerning His glory, we will cease to walk in His way. Once we are not walking in His way, we cause others to stumble. All of this, according to Malachi, corrupts the covenant of Levi, or priesthood.

Listen well to God. Acquire a taste for His glory. Observe and obey His commandments. Cause many to follow your example and claim yours Savior. Covenant with God to be a priest for the world. Be innocent of the crimes for which Malachi accused the priests of his day!

Discussion Questions and Journal Space

1. When was a time God used you effectively in a way that made you realize you are a priest?

2. What do you prioritize more than love in your daily living? What is an action of repentance you can take immediately to change this?

_____

_____

_____

_____

_____

_____

_____

_____

_____

_____

CHAPTER NINE

God's approved priest

Rejecting evil
does not mean you are doing good.

Refusing to be corrupt in our service as a priest is necessary. Still, rejecting evil does not mean you are doing good. As you spend a moment with Malachi, lay your life alongside the standard of a good priest, Levi.

"My covenant with him was a covenant of life and peace, and I gave them to him, that he might hear; and he feared Me, he stood in awe of My name. True instruction was in his mouth, and no wrong was found on his lips. He walked with me in peace and knowledge, and men should seek instruction from his mouth, for he is the messenger of the LORD of hosts." – Malachi 2:5-7

Our lives are not neutral. As we live each day, we commit actions that move people either toward or away from Christ. Consider the importance of this; every person we casually pass will someday be transformed into a creature of radiance or a monster of torture. What we do can be used by God to bring one transformation or the other.

If we desire to glorify Christ, increase our own joy, and reach people, we will seek to be a priest like Levi. Levi spread God's glory. He spread God's truth. He shared God's worth, and he shared God's grace. May God equip us to do the same!

First on our daily to do list must be "spread God's glory." Our daily task is to spread the news that "our God reigns." As believers we have a covenant of life and peace. This covenant allows us not only to have these wonderful gifts, but also to distribute them. We spread God's glory by bringing life and peace to others.

Dead men are walking towards the execution of eternal punishment all around us. We must offer them life. Many war within themselves and with others. We must offer them peace. We spread God's glory when we point to Him as the sole provider of both.

Second, spreading God's truth must become a holy habit of a good priest. The truth of scripture and conviction cannot be compromised in an attempt to give life and peace. It is the truth that sets people free. It may not be popular to speak the truth, but Christ encourages us, "Do not fear those who can harm the body and do nothing to the soul. Fear Him who can kill the body and cast the soul into hell!"

Living as a priest will offend and bless many. All will form a strong opinion about a person spreading God's glory and truth. Some will reject, and some will respect, but certainly all will respond. Living as a priest acts as a wonderful filtering system. You don't have to wonder how people feel about God if you are displaying Him in your life as priest.

Following the example of Levi, Malachi, and most of all, Christ, will not bring regret. No one has lived for Christ and regretted it in their last breath. For sure no one has lived for Christ and regretted after their last breath. He is worth following. Representing him among people is a high and holy aim.

If we could speak to Levi, he would have no regrets. Any suffering or insult is worth the compliment of God. As a priest, Levi had no earthly inheritance. No land was given to the priestly tribe. Their inheritance was God alone. Likewise, today we must reject all earthly rewards that might disqualify us from what is better. A priest longs to hear, "Well done," from the High Priest who employed him. A priest believes the suffering of this age is not worthy to be compared to the glory to come. A priest sells all to gain the Pearl of great price. Let us be priests.

Write a prayer talking to God about your desires to represent Him well as a holy priest.

_____

_____

_____

_____

_____

_____

_____

_____

_____

_____

_____

_____

CHAPTER TEN

An accomplice to sin

"'And now this admonition is for you, O priests. If you do not listen, and if you do not set your heart to honor my name,' says the LORD Almighty, 'I will send a curse upon you, and I will curse your blessings. Yes, I have already cursed them, because you have not set your heart to honor me....You have turned from the way and by your teaching have caused many to stumble; you have violated the covenant.'" - Malachi 2:1-2, 8

More than any other passage in Malachi so far, this passage convicts me of sin. I need to spend several moments with Malachi reflecting on the importance of this passage. More than any other passage, this one brought a moment of genuine repentance. I wish the same for you, not because repentance is fun, but because it is healthy.

When I first examined this passage, I repented of leading my congregation with a false assumption. Many of them had come to me confessing sins and struggles. I had listened, prayed, even cried with them.

I had sinned, however, because I told them over and over again that it was a long process to overcome sin. I encouraged them to be patient. Malachi wouldn't have said that. God doesn't instruct that. I shouldn't have said that.

What I should have done is look them in the eye, and with full confidence and compassion, tell them, "You don't have to sin like that anymore." Does this seem harsh? Jesus didn't tell the woman caught in adultery to go as many days as she could without sinning like that again, but I had said this to someone who dealt with sexual sin. Jesus didn't tell her that recovery would be a slow process and she should be patient with herself, but I had said that to someone with temper problems. Jesus looked at her with confidence and compassion and commanded, "Go and sin no more."

Repentance was necessary because I had been an accomplice to their sin. I was sinning the same way these priests rebuked by Malachi sinned. The priests were not guilty directly of bringing sorry sacrifices, but they were guilty of allowing others to bring sorry sacrifices. There was a direct parallel with their sins and my own.

Under the new covenant, our lives are the sacrifices we offer to Christ. We are commanded in Romans 12:1 to "offer our bodies as living sacrifices, holy and pleasing to God–this is your spiritual act of worship." All we do is to be done with the intent to glorify Christ by impacting people.

When another believer comes to you and shares their struggles with sin, they are sharing their struggle to keep their sacrifices pure. A pure and holy response will not take the situation too lightly. The priests sinned   because they saw sorry sacrifices and looked the other way. I had sinned with equal wickedness because when my congregants opened up, and showed me their sacrifices, I spoke of God's forgiveness without speaking of God's holiness. I had misrepresented God because He does not look the other way.

Of course, God casts our sins as far as the east is from the west. But equal to that, He promises to give us strength to conquer our sins. We must be the face of Jesus to each other, and we must have the boldness to say in love, "Don't sin anymore!"

I have soundly repented of my failure, and God has completely forgiven me. He has strengthened me to share the wonderful truth that you don't have to sin anymore. God offers more than forgiveness. He offers us strength to meet His holy requirements.

When you are struggling with temptation, you don't have to think only about how great God's forgiveness is going to be the second after you sin. You should consider instead how great God's holiness is that very second. You should meditate on how great your sin would insult that holiness.

Malachi urges us not to forget how large God's power is. You and I can avoid sin. We have a lopsided representation of Christ when we advertise Him as faithful to forgive our sin (First John 1:9), without also proclaiming Him as faithful to keep us from sinning (1st Corinthians 10:13). Both are legs that keep us walking on the straight and narrow.

You are not just responsible for your own living. You have a holy and hard responsibility to rebuke those who are sinning. Genuine love covers sin not by ignoring it, but by confronting it. God is holy and loving, but each attribute is abstract unless in relationship with us. Refuse to be an accomplice to sin.

Discussion Questions and Journal Space

1. Do you do you count on Jesus' forgiveness after sin more than His power available during temptation?

2. How have you let people off the hook, so to speak, instead of rebuking them about some repetitive sin?

_____

_____

_____

_____

_____

_____

_____

_____

_____

CHAPTER ELEVEN

We are family

God is global, but He is also relational.
He desires to reach all the nations
as well as knit together
the hearts of every local church.

When my dad turned fifty, all his kids were there. My brother flew in from New York City. My pregnant-with-triplets sister drove up from Houston. For almost five hours we honored a man who had shaped our lives. The synergy of the siblings easily stimulated appreciation for dad.

God is global, but He is also relational. He desires to reach all the nations as well as knit together the hearts of every local church. We are family. The Christian life is a communal life. Like at my dad's party, our heavenly Father is honored much when we're united. Malachi's community hadn't come together in a long time.

"Do we not all have one father? Has not one God created us? Why do we deal treacherously with each against his brother so as to profane the covenant of our fathers? Judah has dealt treacherously, and an abomination has been committed in Israel and in Jerusalem; for Judah has profaned the sanctuary of the Lord which He loves and has married the daughter of a foreign god." – Malachi 2:10-11

A moment with Malachi today will be good medicine for our relationships. Maybe, for you, these words will be preventive. You will need to remember them and allow them to protect your heart from division. These words could also be prescriptive. Maybe, you need to receive them as vitamins to help fight the sickness of disunity you have. Either way, as you take a moment with Malachi, hear these words.

We all have the same Father. This is supposed to be enough for us to be globally and locally connected. This similarity should be large enough for us to get along. I can't say I don't have much in common with another Christian when we have the same Father in heaven.

These Jews had forgotten they shared the same adoption story. They were brothers and sisters. They belonged to the same culture. We must remember this as well. What unites a culture is that they have the same story. This is why Christianity is a culture, and we share an adoption story.

Imagine two orphans talking during lunch. One says, "My dad rescued me from a debt I could never have paid."

The other answers, "So did my dad."

"Oh yeah," begins the first orphan, "Well my dad sent His oldest Son to change my way of life."

"Mine too," says orphan number two. "My dad is coming back for me one day, and I'll live with him and His first son, Jesus."

"Hey," exclaims the second orphan, "My dad's coming back for me and my older brother's name is Jesus too."

Once the orphans realize they have the same father there will be a connection not shared by all those other orphans. This is how it should be with us. We must remember we have the same dad so we'll have love for our siblings.

I have two sons, Miles and Miller. They add much joy to my life, but can add pain as well. The greatest pain comes when they don't get along. They are young now, but one day they may argue fiercely; maybe they'll even say they hate each other.

In that moment I will be hurt more than they. I'll want to grab them and say, "Don't you know you have the same father and mother. Aren't we a big enough part of your lives to stimulate fellowship?" We can only image the insult and pain we cause God when we don't unite with brothers and sisters in Christ. Having the same dad should be big enough to stimulate unity within the church.

Having the same Father unites us under the same covenant. Here's where we get into some heavy stuff. Wrap your heart and mind around this - the way Judah had acted treacherously against Israel didn't have anything to do with how Judah was treating Israel directly. Judah acted treacherously by going off and marrying a pagan wife.

God's people are so connected that our unity is not just hurt by the way we treat each other, but by the way we live independently, or least we think it's independently. The way you treat one person in my family affects the relationship you have with my entire family. This truth is maximized in the context of the family of God.

Covenants knit us together. Whether the old covenant or the new covenant, what one person does affects all others in the covenant. Your church is a covenant community, an organism where no member is mutually exclusive to another.

The great Red Oaks of California tower over those who walk in their forests. Dozens of men still can't ring around the thickness of some trees. What is unseen, below the soil from which the trees shoot, is an amazing display of connection. The roots of one tree tangle into the roots of another until it's impossible to trace them back to the original owner.

We are connected at our roots as well. Our deepest story is redemption. A moment with Malachi encourages us not to fear the soil of venerability. Growing strong and tall will more likely occur in an interconnected community sharing roots.

Discussion Questions and Journal Space

1. How might your living be affecting others who love you? How does their living affect you?

2. Why do you think we are tempted to suppose that our actions don't connect with those around us? What specific form of repentance can you take to better remind yourself of your connection to your family and church and world?

_____

_____

_____

_____

_____

_____

_____

CHAPTER TWELVE

Six Similarities

Our actions are not just our own, but determine the blessings of God upon another.

Unity is important enough to take two moments for celebration and discovery. Our actions are not just our own, but determine the blessings of God upon another. Sharing the same covenant means we have at least six similarities, similarities that deeply connect us to each other, like roots intertwined.

We are united in sin. The first military battle Israel lost was because one man sinned. God told Joshua to attack Ai, but not to take any spoil. He did this from time to time to send a message, "You don't need their stuff. You have

Me." One man, Achan, stole a golden vase, and for the first time the Israel army suffered casualties.

God didn't just say, "Okay Achan, you're dead." Achan's sin caused others to die. Likewise, your sins and mine affect our entire community. When you sin against God, you block His blessing upon all of us. You should be encouraging others to live right not just for their sake, but for your sake as well.

We are united in faith. There's a story you probably remember about Jesus teaching in a crowded house and four people bringing their paralyzed friend to Him through the roof. The Bible reports that, "When Jesus saw their faith, He said to the paralyzed man, 'Be healed.'"

That's huge. Nothing is mentioned about the sick man's faith. The faith of his friends was enough. Likewise, in community, you can have faith for me, and I can have faith for you. Some of the rewards you get have nothing to do with your individual faith. You are getting blessed for the faith your community has.

We are united in joy. The destiny of every person is to stand before Jesus. To some He will say, "Depart from Me you worker of iniquity, I never knew you." To others He will say, "Well done, My good and faithful servant. Enter the joy prepared for you." Christ invites us to enter His joy. That's the legacy of community. If we are like Christ, we will be inviting people to enter our joy.

We are united in suffering. Have you ever heard, "I know Jesus won't give me more than I can bear?" That's a lie! Of course He gives you more than you can bear. I know where people get that saying; it comes from 1st Corinthians 10:13 where we are told God won't tempt us past what we are able. The verse is about temptation, not suffering. All of us are given loads of suffering past what we are capable of carrying.

This happens so we will ask others to help us. We can carry our loads together. We are stronger in community than as added up individuals. We are stronger together and should be carrying each other's load.

We are united in worship. Jesus said in the Sermon on the Mount, "If you come to the altar and there remember you have something against your brother – leave your gift there and go. First be reconciled with your brother and then come and offer your gift."

Those are surprising words from Jesus. No other religion values community so much. I wonder how many believers who gather each week are guilty of breaking this command. Jesus says you worship best in unity. We can't celebrate our dad unless we are right with our siblings.

Finally, we are united in love. We love each other because there is a part of us that comes to life when we're together. When we don't see someone, part of us dies that only comes to life when they are with us. We miss people partly because we miss who we are when we're with them.

Are you contributing to the unity of your family? Do you stimulate love among those in your church? We all have the same Dad and are part of the same covenant. We should be intimately wrapped up in each other's lives.

We sin together. We have faith together. We share our joys and our sorrows with each other. We worship together. We love each other. This is the reality of Christian living. There are others on the straight and narrow path, and we walk it best when we lock arms and unite hearts.

Discussion Questions and Journal Space

1. Of the six similarities, which do you hold most dear and why?
2. Which similarity brings your heart closest to those you love?

CHAPTER THIRTEEN

Covenant keeping is cultural

Being Christian is a way of life.

We are part of the same family. We share the same covenant. This joins every believer in a culture called Christianity. The Christian faith is not an academic mindset or merely a belief system. Being a Christian is a way of life. It means you belong to a particular culture, the culture of Christianity.

Let me give you a test. The test is called, "Are you more Christian or American?" There are three questions.

1. Which do you think is more honorable, dying for your country on a battlefield or dying for your faith on a mission field?

2. Which do you think is more important, the increase of your pocket book or the increase of your prayer life?

3. Which do you dream most of achieving, the American dream (a good spouse, a good career, two cars, and a 1.5 kids) or the Great Commission (reaching all the ethnic groups for Christ)?

If you are mostly American, I hope this moment with Malachi can jolt you into a better culture. There is no culture better than Christianity. Christianity is a culture because it is a way of life. More than gender, more than race, more than economic status, Christian faith should define who you are.

People usually marry within their culture. As a matter of fact, cultural anthropologists use that variable to define what culture a person believes they are part. Before Christ overwhelms someone and changes their culture, they usually marry strictly within the same race, age, religion, and/or economic status.

When it comes to God defining marriage, He commands what Christians may think they already practice. He demands marrying within the culture. According to God, however, our culture is Christianity. The reality of having Christ in our lives makes race, age, previous religion, and economic status small in comparison.

In *Fiddler on the Roof*, a Jewish father named Tevye sees three of his daughters married. The first wants to marry outside the family's economic status and without a matchmaker. Tavye reluctantly agrees because they are in love. The second wants to marry beyond their political opinion and without his permission. He barely agrees to this.

Tevye's first daughter is married to a poor tailor, and his second is married to a communist. Then the third daughter desires to marry outside of their religious faith. Tevye's reaction expresses well the reaction Malachi had to the same issue. With a broken heart and twisted face, he shouts "No!" Earlier Tevye had advised, "A bird may love a fish, but where would they build a home?"

"Judah has broken faith. A detestable thing has been committed in Israel and in Jerusalem: Judah has desecrated the sanctuary the LORD loves, by marrying the daughter of a foreign god. As for the man who does this, whoever he may be, may the LORD cut him off from the tents of Jacob -even though he brings offerings to the LORD Almighty."
- Malachi 2:11-13

It was the strategy of Alexander the Great to kill cultures through forced marriages. The strategy, though effective, was not original. Our great enemy has been attacking the culture of

Christianity for years with marriages that cause God to yell "no."

Malachi pleads with us to remember our covenant so we won't forget our culture. Once we forget our covenant with God and others, we easily abandoned who we are. This can lead to marrying outside the faith, a sin greatly damaging the fabric of our communities.

God wants us to prepare for and enjoy a wonderful, intimate, affair-proof, divorce-proof marriage. You can start preparing for that marriage now. If we follow the instructions of Malachi we will have more joy in marriage, in family, in life. It all begins with remembering our covenant and practicing our culture.

God doesn't suggest you marry only a believer. He demands it with aggression. If you marry an unbeliever, you break your faith. Every sin doesn't have equal consequence. They are all equal in that they insult God, and they can be forgiven, but I would much rather be lied to than shot. Likewise, marrying an unbeliever has deep and long-term consequences.

When you marry an unbeliever you throw away your faith for personal liberty. God calls this detestable. He also says it desecrates the sanctuary which the LORD loves. The sanctuary is the congregation. The entire community is damaged when someone marries outside the culture of faith. The punishment mentioned in Malachi is for the man to be cut off from Judah, even if he continues to bring offerings to the Lord.

This is not only a Jewish, Old Testament command. In the New Testament, Paul instructs believers not to be unequally yoked. "Yoked" means joined together for a common task. A yoke was a figure eight, which would join two oxen as they pulled a plow. If a farmer unequally yoked the oxen, it would be almost impossible to plow a straight line. Also, the stronger ox would begin to pull the weight of the weaker, quickly becoming exhausted.

Do you see the parallel? When you are joined together with an unbeliever you will find it nearly impossible to walk the straight and narrow path of Christian culture. You will tire easily because you won't have help from your partner.

God wants you to be loved deeply by your spouse, but this is impossible if you marry outside the faith. First John 1:7-8 says that anyone who loves is of God and whoever doesn't love is not of God because God is love. A lost person cannot love as deeply as a believer because they do not have God, who is Love. I don't mean that lost people can't care, but they won't sacrifice for the sake of their partner as willingly or often as a saved person. Lost people have never surrendered their life to the God of love.

We have a responsibility to make the world a better place. We are to spread God's grace and glory in ways that have global implications. This often seems a daunting task. Think however, if we simply raised our children to see Christianity as a way of life, rather than just a belief system, how the world would quickly change, and for the better.

Discussion Questions and Journal Space

1. How does the sin of marrying outside the faith continue to impact people's lives after the wedding ceremony?

2. If God demands we don't marry outside the faith, why do you think Christians are sometimes attracted to people who are lost? Is this a sin?

_____

_____

_____

_____

_____

_____

_____

CHAPTER FOURTEEN

Great sex

No one approves of sex more than God

God created sex. He even commands it. God's plan is for us to remember the covenant relationship we have with Him and others, practice the culture of Christianity by marrying others in the covenant of faith, and have strong marriages. He has given the gift of sex to help fulfill this purpose.

Most women desire to be beautiful and most men desire to be strong. These desires can become reality in a relationship of healthy sexual relations. Some of you may not need a moment with Malachi today since you are married and enjoy this gift already. For others, I hope today's moment will increase your resolve to save yourself for a gift worth the waiting.

Sex is a serious activity. It is a covenant. Covenants have three major truths; they are ordained by God, they are activated by agreement, and they include blood. God ordained sex. It becomes a wonderful part of the marriage commitment when the two getting married agree to wait until marriage to have sex.

When God rescued Adam from death, He spilt the blood from animals. When God called out Israel as a special nation, He commanded them to sacrifice animals. When God extended grace to all peoples, the blood of His only Son flowed from the cross.

Having sex for the first time on the marriage night is to be placed among other covenant events. Through blood God announces, "I have rescued you from loneliness. I have called you to each other. I have extended to you My grace!" God celebrates His plan, and He is angry when it's violated.

Waiting to have sex until marriage is the ultimate test of genuine love; love for God and love for the person. When you have sex with someone before God allows, you have replaced God with a human idol. Instead of the sex being an act of worship and obedience, it is an insult. Your sex is a gesture toward God that says, "I do not love You more than I love this person and my own animal instincts."

Not only that, but when you have sex before marriage, you are communicating to your sexual partner you don't genuinely love them. Love wants what's best for another person. How many Christians have had unlawful sex sacrificially, as a gift to another that says, "I know this is the best thing for you"?

Love is patient. Lust is not patient. Hormones are not patient. When you have sex early in the name of love, you are redefining love. You are not saying that God is love, because you are not giving God to that person. You are not saying love is patient because you are not being patient with that person. You are creating definitions that don't exist in order to justify your sin.

The best way to avoid the sin of having sex before marriage is to know exactly what your boundaries are and make them stricter than you think necessary. Some people should not be alone with anyone from the opposite sex until marriage. Some people should stop at holding hands. Some people should do no more than kiss. Certainly second, third, and home base are only for married people.

The path to sexual purity involves God. Knowing God will lead to sexual purity. "Knowing," in Biblical language, means to enter into in an intimate way. Sometimes we read in scripture, "he knew her, and she had a child."

To know God means to allow Him to enter you in an intimate way – not a sexual way, of course, but an intimate way, even a romantic way. God doesn't command you to avoid romance. Just as He led Eve to Adam, he will lead you to your spouse. The more you know Him, the greater sexual purity you'll have.

If you know God, you'll have a view of Him as powerful, holy, and satisfying. So when you are tempted with pornography or masturbation or sex outside of marriage, you'll conquer that sin. You will think, "God is powerful enough to deliver me. God is holy enough to be very angry if I don't allow Him to deliver me. God is satisfying enough to keep me from regretting I didn't sin, but instead chose obedience."

Please be open for this joy. Remember you are not called to be an American. You are not to surrender to the values of this world. You are called to be a Christian. This fact casts a shadow over every other variable of your identity. Make Malachi 2:11-13 words that don't describe you so you can hear other words from Jesus that do - "Well done, My good and faithful servant."

"Judah has broken faith. A detestable thing has been committed in Israel and in Jerusalem: Judah has desecrated the sanctuary the LORD loves, by

marrying the daughter of a foreign god. As for the man who does this, whoever he may be, may the LORD cut him off from the tents of Jacob -even though he brings offerings to the LORD Almighty."

Discussion Questions and Journal Space

1. How do you feed the lust of your flesh? Are you willing to repent in order to please Jesus?

2. Have you ever thought of sex being tied to covenant and worship? How can you honor God with sex or lack of it?

_____

_____

_____

_____

_____

CHAPTER FIFTEEN

Theology matters

"Another thing you do: You flood the LORD's altar with tears. You weep and wail because he no longer pays attention to your offerings or accepts them with pleasure from your hands. ^{14} You ask, "Why?" It is because the LORD is acting as the witness between you and the wife of your youth, because you have broken faith with her, though she is your partner, the wife of your marriage covenant." – Malachi 2:13-14

Theology is a collection of thoughts about God. A comprehensive theology will never exist, but still theology is incredibly important. Our view of God is the most important view we have because from it stems all our other views. Behind your behaviors you'll find your desires. Behind your desires you'll find your theology.

These priests weren't living righteously. They were having sexual affairs. They hadn't left their wives because Malachi says "she is your partner," but they had broken their covenant vow. Whether through neglect or abuse, they turned away from their bride. A moment with Malachi will show how faulty theology corrupted these priests. It will do the same to you and me if we allow it.

These priests thought God could be tricked into forgiving them if they gave some great emotional display at the altar. They believed that God passed out forgiveness lightly.

All sin starts with a bad view of who God is. It is impossible to sin while meditating on greatness and holiness and brilliance of God. Remember, your view of God is the most important view you have because from it comes every other view.

Even an atheist who says there is no God, or wishes there were no God, lives from that view. When your view of God is that He doesn't exist or does not care, you'll live like an atheist. Your theology matters.

These priests viewed God as small. They didn't view Him as all knowing. They didn't view Him as wise. They didn't view Him as holy. This led them to misunderstand repentance.

We should fill our heads with wonderful truths about God. Truths concerning His vastness and splendor and power and grace should be deposited into our minds through study. Like any relationship, knowing about the person increases our understanding of the person and helps us better relate.

Wonderful thoughts about God should be so heavy within us that they sink in to our hearts, turning into worship. The renewing of our minds will lead to the rejoicing of our hearts. Theology turns to doxology. We say factually, "This is the day that the Lord has made." Then it is only natural to say, "Let us rejoice and be glad in it."

Rejoicing then turns to ministry. God is so great that He must be shared. So the mind falls into the heart, and the heart falls into the feet. Our service is stimulated by our love, and our love is fueled by our theology. Fuel your service with study. Talking moments with Malachi should lead to taking walks toward those with needs. Read, then sing, then serve, all the while refusing to forget, theology matters.

Write some simple and great truths you believe with all your heart and then how those truths connect to your emotions.

_____

_____

_____

_____

_____

_____

CHAPTER SIXTEEN

Repentance is obedience

Genuine repentance may or may not involve emotion, but it always involves change.

Better theology might have led to genuine repentance for these previously mentioned priests. Instead, a bad view of God led to a wrong view of repentance. These priests were sinning greatly, allowing sorry sacrifices and hiding sexual affairs. Then they were praying with great emotion, assuming they had gained forgiveness.

"... you cover the altar of the LORD with tears, with weeping and with groaning, because He no longer regards the offering or accepts it with favor from your hand."- Malachi 2:13

115

They were flooding the altar with tears. Any human who witnessed this would have assumed genuine repentance was occurring. But God was not meeting with them because He measures genuine repentance differently than humans. With God, repentance means obedience. A moment with Malachi today should stimulate both.

Genuine repentance may or may not involve emotion, but it always involves change. Check your heart. Do you try to gain forgiveness from God with action other than repentance? I think we have all been guilty of this. We give money to try to gain forgiveness. We read the Bible trying to gain forgiveness. We go on mission trips to gain forgiveness. We might even cry on our faces, like these priests, with hopes to buy forgiveness with our tears. Nothing gains forgiveness except repentance.

These priests certainly regretted what they had done. Regret, however, is not repentance. Regret is the guilt you feel when you are caught. Regret is not a hatred of sin but shame from the results of sin. Much regret does not gain any forgiveness.

One year I taught debate at a high school and had several students plagiarize an essay. Since I didn't grade the papers immediately, it was about two weeks before I discovered the crime. When I confronted the class, they hung their heads in shame. Many of them said they were really sorry.

One student in particular gave much effort to gain a clear conscience. He redid the paper. He told me he was sorry everyday. He said he lost sleep for three nights. He did this because he really wanted to be eligible for the school's competitive play in which he had a role.

He didn't care about restoring a relationship with me – I was just a teacher he'd forget during summer. He wanted to get a grade from me that would keep him eligible for an activity he enjoyed.

The priests Malachi rebuked enjoyed being priests. They had status and power. They were crying out for that more than to be restored to God. They didn't want to repent. They wanted to live in sin and enjoy the gifts of obedience. I hope you are not like them.

Notice: No emotional display, no courageous evangelism, no amount of money given – NO THING – will gain you forgiveness. Repentance is the only door to forgiveness. All other efforts to gain forgiveness will leave us frustrated because God will stay silent.

To repent means to turn around. The primary evidence of repentance is change. If drinking Mountain Dew is a sin, and I tell you I have repented, it means I've quit drinking Mountain Dew. Of course, we can't repent in our own strength, but God is powerful enough to turn us around. Repentance means to walk away from our sin, toward God. No one can walk toward both at the same time.

God said to these priests, "I have the power you want, and My plan is to give it to you when you plan to use it to stop sinning. I will not forgive you just so you can feel better." We must experience the wonderful truth these priests had ignored. God's grace does not only come after you sin. God's grace can come before you sin. God's grace can keep you from sinning.

Imagine grace as a pill you take. The medicine doesn't just serve as an antibiotic, but also as a steroid. When we take God's grace into our lives, He doesn't just kill sin. He strengthens us with supernatural power to avoid sin. Too many times we only want half the pill. We want past sins erased, but not future ones.

God, the Great Physician, commanded the priests to take all their medicine or get none of it at all. Have you been guilty of wanting God's grace as a painkiller but not a steroid? Repentance gains God's full pardon, and with that pardon comes power. The same grace that cleanses us after the sin can strengthen us before the sin.

If you have committed to share the gospel with someone, but haven't done it yet, the only repentance is to actually go and share. If you commit to read your Bible, and then at the end of the day remember you haven't – don't pray for forgiveness, just get up and read.

Only through repentance will you gain grace from God. This grace will erase your sin and will empower you not to sin like that anymore. The righteous living that follows is evidence of repentance. Continuing to choose the same sin over and over again means God's grace has not been gained, which means true repentance hasn't occurred, which means you are living in sin.

Come to Jesus the way you initially came, with faith that He can conquer all your sin. You first came to Jesus for forgiveness of your sin (singular), and you knew that gaining that forgiveness meant a lifestyle change. Have the same faith when dealing with your sins (plural). Every individual sin can be conquered the same way our sin was conquered, by grace, through faith in Jesus.

Plan to actually repent. Write down a sin you know you have, then how you will repent of that sin, then perform the repentance right now. Make a call, return a stolen item, write a check giving generously, tell someone you're sorry – whatever it takes to actually repent, do it now and bask in God's pleasure.

CHAPTER SEVENTEEN

Where is the God of justice?

God gives a sharp rebuke to those who believe they deserve justice rather than desiring to spread justice to others.

God is not bound to us or our ideas of justice. Before He acts, He does not check with us for approval. The only committee making decisions of global implications is the Trinity. The Jews of Malachi's day would disagree. They wondered where the God of justice was hiding since their lives seemed to be so terrible. They assumed any suffering they endured was unjust.

Many continue to make the same assumption. In self-pity we sometimes ask the question of these Jews, "Where is the God of justice?" We must find an answer to this question or we risk wearying the Lord with our words. Taking a moment with Malachi to discover the answer may show that we've overlooked the obvious.

You have wearied the LORD with your words. "How have we wearied him?" you ask. By saying, "All who do evil are good in the eyes of the LORD, and he is pleased with them" or "Where is the God of justice?" - Malachi 2:17

If God is not just, then He is not God. The God of justice is the only true god there really is. Putting God's justice on trial is the same as trying God Himself. This is what these Jews were doing, questioning the very character of God because they did not feel they were getting enough out of Him. They were really fighting for favors, not justice.

Complaining that life is not fair and asking God to send us comfort is not an attitude that pleases Christ. God gives a sharp rebuke to those who believe they deserve justice rather   than desiring to spread justice to others. Make sure you are a distributor of justice.

God responds to this question with a rebuke, *"Behold, I send My messenger, and he will prepare the way before Me. And the Lord, whom you seek, will suddenly come to His temple."*

These words from God begin encouragingly enough, but take a sharp turn. *"But who can endure the day of His coming? And who can stand when He appears? He will purify and purge."* Asking for justice is a fearful thing because sometimes it is we who need punishment so justice can be served.

So where is the God of justice? He is in the future waiting to send justice upon all, including the religious. There will come a day when all will be set right. When we complain, "it just isn't fair," we are really saying, "God doesn't seem to know what He is doing." We should remember, all will be right in due time.

Still, one great sweep of future justice is surely not the only place justice will be served. Today, in the present we must be able to find the God of justice somewhere, but where? Let's consider three men who stood for justice, then answer this important question.

Consider first of all John the Baptizer, the messenger God mentioned in today's text. John stood for justice when he rebuked Herod for marrying his brother's wife. Why would the Baptizer dabble in politics? Couldn't he have continued preaching and baptizing if he conveniently ignored Herod's sin?

Also reflect upon the ministry of Martin Luther King, Jr. King stood for justice when he joined the bus boycott Rosa Parks unknowingly stimulated. A pastor of a church, he certainly had tasks to complete. His actions followed his own advice, "Do not think to yourself, 'What will happen to me if I help this person?' Ask, 'what will happen to this person if I do not help.'"

Jesus Christ, of course, can be added to the list of those aiming to spread justice. Not content to lead His apostles in a bubble of comfort, He stands against the crime of selling sacrifices in the temple.

There are three similarities shared by these three men. All of them had "main" ministries, but refused to use that as an excuse for not standing for justice. Also, all of them ended up dying largely due to their stand for justice. Most compelling, each knew the answer to the question, "Where is the God of justice?"

Certainly God waits in the future to bring final justice. Right now, however, the God of justice resides in His people. When we ask, "God, why are You not doing something to stop that injustice?" He may respond, "I could ask you the same question." God is within us; we carry the God of justice within our heart. If it is justice we want, we have only to release Him, even if it costs us our life.

Discussion Questions and Journal Space

1. Do you too often lean towards convenience rather than justice when facing a chance to right a wrong?

2. Do you spend more time spreading justice to others or trying to claim it for yourself?

_____

_____

_____

_____

_____

_____

_____

_____

_____

_____

CHAPTER EIGHTEEN

Painful purification

We do not worship God as if He needs it.
God can adequately celebrate Himself.

That God desires to spread justice to the world through us is amazing. Even more amazing, God does not use us as mere pawns in His global quest. He wants to have a relationship with us. The greatest expression of this relationship is worship. The painful process of improving our worship is purification.

"He is like a refiner's fire and like fullers' soap. He will sit as a smelter and purifier of silver, and He will purify the sons of Levi and refine them like gold and silver, so that they may present to the LORD offerings in righteousness. Then the offering of Judah and Jerusalem will be pleasing to

the LORD as in the days of old and as in former years." Malachi 3:2-4

Few volunteer for pain. Desiring pain for pain's sake is a mental illness. There is pain involved, however, in many of life's pursuits. Often times, moving toward a prize involves pain, but the pain makes the prize even more desirable. This is the case when the prize is God.

God loves to be worshiped. As we praise Him, He is delighted, and we are satisfied. What we need most for our spiritual well being is to see God. What God wants most for our spiritual well being is to reveal Himself. It's a wonderful match, and its zenith is worship in spirit and truth.

We do not worship God as if He needs it. God promises to purify Malachi's audience not because He is lonely. He promises to purify as a gift so that they may bring good offerings. God can adequately celebrate Himself. God can have rocks cry out His praises. What God prefers is for us to travel the painful road of purification so that we can celebrate our greatest prize, Christ.

As much as God desires, even demands to be worshiped, He will not lower His standard of holiness to gain our praise. God is completely holy. His love beckons us to come, but His holiness refuses anything less than a pure offering. The tension between God's love and holiness created a great dilemma.

Malachi looked around to see few caring about God. Few desired to worship Him. God's holiness demands that, for His glory's sake, these evildoers die swiftly. God's love, however, demands their rescue. The answer to this tension is purification.

Purification offers pain and improvement to satisfy God's holiness. Purification increases intimacy and depth of relationship to satisfy God's love. The ultimate expression of purification is seen in the cross of Jesus.

Jesus took pain we were unable to bear. The entire cup of wrath was poured upon Him so that no one could argue against God's holiness. God is certainly holy because He dealt thoroughly with sin upon the cross. Likewise, the embrace of love is extended through the cross. None can contend God does not love for God so loved the world that He offered His only begotten Son. Upon the cross, holiness and love marry.

We take up our cross and follow Christ into greater holiness and greater love. The means of gaining glory and enabling us to live righteously is painful. God may give constant irritations that scratch our souls as a way of producing pearls displaying His worth. He may give long-term pressure upon our hearts as a way of producing diamonds that display His splendor. In today's moment with Malachi, however, He mentions purifying us as gold, with fire.

When someone purifies gold they first mine it out of filth. The valuable metal is mixed with soil and cheap rock. Since gold is dense, when melted all together in a pot, the filth will float to the surface, and the purifier will scrap it away. Over and over again, the heat will increase and the scum will be discarded.

God doesn't burn us just for the burning's sake. He desires to look into a golden soul and see His face reflected. There is much scum to be scrapped and discarded. Purification is painful because we have merged our hearts with filth.

How easily we forget that we are at war. Our very soul is a battlefield. Satan pulls as God hold us tightly. In the process our soul is stretched, and we find more room for God to take residence. Pain is not a healthy pursuit for its own sake, but gaining more of God allows us to rejoice a bit as our soul gets stretched.

As we move toward Christ with hopes of worshiping Him better, we will experience pain. There will be times of silence from God. There will be times of insults from people. There will be times of sickness, persecution, and confusion. There is no reason to pretend we enjoy or understand these times.

Faith is the evidence of things unseen. Time after time suffering blinds us to God's goodness. In the dark flames of purification we must have faith to believe that they are nothing in comparison to the glory awaiting us. We need not thank God for suffering, but must thank God during suffering for being God. He is stretching our soul in order to pour more of Himself into our lives. Our worship is richer with wounds.

Discussion Questions and Journal Space

1. How much better would your life be if you realized you've already gain the greatest treasure, God Himself? What would be different in your daily living if you viewed God as a treasure?

2. When was there a time that pain opened up more space for God to reign in your life?

CHAPTER NINETEEN

Responding to the fire

Jesus is our example. Jesus wept.

Yesterday, during a moment with Malachi, only one side of the coin was examined. We considered the purification of our soul through suffering allowed by God. Two clarifications are now needed. First, purification can come through means other than suffering. Second, sometimes we observe the suffering purification of others and should know how to respond appropriately.

Our response to the judgment of God upon others should match the response of Malachi. He refused to blame God, and he refused to abandon his people. When we see the fire of God purifying others, we should do the same.

Truth does not eliminate compassion. Far too often we are conditioned to think belief in God's sovereignty disqualifies us to display Christ's compassion. Malachi does well declaring God's power while being emotional with those God desired to purify.

Jeremiah did the same thing. Reading his prophetic book followed by his lament powerfully shows how truth and passion can mix. Jeremiah preaches the truth of God's judgment coming upon the people of Judah, but when it comes, he doesn't say, "I told you so." Instead, Jeremiah weeps and wails at the judgment of God. He cries for those who have lost loved ones. Believing that pain purifies, he still cries with the hurting.

Jesus, as always, is the best example. "Jesus wept." The Greek expression would include bouncing shoulders and audible groans. Jesus loved Mary and Martha and wept with them at the loss of their brother even though He knew the truth – Lazarus would be alive in minutes.

During a particular suffering in my life, dozens of people gave me truth when I desperately longed for compassion. Our second child, still in the womb, was considered to be in grave danger. We were given a fifty-fifty chance and two weeks to wait. The waiting was filled with those who meant well telling us, "God has a plan," and "God's in control." No one wept with us.

Jesus practiced what he preached, "Do unto others what you would have them do unto you." When going through a time of suffering purification, are there any who want insult added to injury? The fire of God is fair, but we need not point that out to those suffering in its flames. We need not point at all, but rather embrace. Powerful theology can be invisible theology supporting involved ministry.

We must dare to get into the pot and feel the heat. We are to weep with those who weep and laugh with those who laugh. Interestingly, we tend to do the opposite. We attempt to cheer up those crying and bring down those laughing. We desire people to adjust their emotions to us rather than obeying Scripture and following the example of Jesus.

Malachi carries the burden of the Lord. He is not being purified through suffering in flames but through ministering to those who are. There are other ways to stretch our souls than God's fire.

Let us resolve to be disciplined towards our own soul. We must prune ourselves through repentance, reducing the fuel for God's fire when it comes. In short, we must surrender now what God will burn later. Responding correctly to the suffering of others is one way to do this.

Discussion Questions and Journal Space

1. What can you surrender now that God will want to remove from your life with fire later? Will you?

2. How often do you grieve with those who grieve? Do you usually try to pull them out of sorrow and pain or enter into it with them so you can come out together?

_____

_____

_____

_____

_____

_____

_____

_____

_____

_____

Chapter Twenty

Returning

God has decided to love us, and He cannot,
and will not change. When we sin, we are
not destroyed. Instead, we are invited to
have our sins cast as far as the
east is from the west.

Every second God accomplishes more than the entire world could do in their combined lifetimes. If we could freeze a second and examine the tasks of God, we'd need an eternity to do so. Yet God would not consider Himself busy, and He never gets so tired He needs sleep. We have an amazing God.

Right now, this very second, God is keeping in check the gravitation force of every star, planet, and moon. He makes sure, each and every second, that the earth doesn't shoot out into the cold, dark abyss. He is setting the temperature everywhere all at once.

This second, God is pulling in the tide at once place and pushing it back in another. Now, God sets the sun here as he raises the sun there. He begins the song of the crickets on one side of the globe while morning larks sing on the other side. He manages hurricanes, earthquakes, tornadoes, volcanoes, and avalanches.

This is not to say that all God does is manage the physical world. No, He is personally involved in the lives of us all. Right now, this very second, God says to thousands, "Depart from Me," as He says to thousands more, "Well done, My good and faithful servant."

God mourns an abortion, and He celebrates a birth. He is saddened and angered by divorce while smiling upon all the holy matrimonies. God is able to have a million tasks at once, feel a million emotions at once, and hear a million prayers at once - all as if He is only doing one thing! We have an amazing God.

What is particularly amazing is that this God, who does all of the above and more each second, includes you in His daily tasks. Along with checking the water level of the ocean and controlling the plates in the earth's crust, God extends an invitation.

"'For I am the LORD, I do not change; therefore you are not consumed, O sons of Jacob. Yet from the days of your fathers you have gone away from My ordinances and have not kept them. Return to Me, and I will return to you,' says the LORD of hosts. But you said, 'In what way shall we return?'" – Malachi 3:6-7

God does not need human companionship. He has never been lonely. For an eternity past He enjoyed wonderful and intimate fellowship Himself. The Father loves the Son, the Son loves the Father, and the Spirit loves them both as they also love the Spirit. Humans were created because there was such an overflow of love between the Triune Members. Our job is to position ourselves under God and allow the overflow to fall upon us.

Even though these Jews Malachi ministers to had sinned greatly, God gives them permission to return to Him. We have the same invitation. "Come, all you who are heavy laden and receive rest. Come, though your sins be as scarlet they will be made white as snow. Come, fetch the fatted calf, My child has returned." God loves to have us return to Him.

God has decided to love us, and He cannot and will not change. When we sin, we are not destroyed. Instead, we are invited to have our sins cast as far as the east is from the west. God, capable of anything, agrees to forget our sins when we return to Him.

There is no evidence that these Jews returned to God. The hypocrisy and rebellion cultivated instead into the Pharisee sect we read about in the Gospels. They put their faith in religion instead of returning to God. The result, four hundred years of silence when God did not speak through His prophets.

We should greatly fear what might happen if we fail to return to God. We will not stay spiritually stagnant. Our rebellion will grow worse and worse. Our children's children will be greater sinners than we if we do not return. Also, as we continue to sin, God's voice will become softer and softer. If we do not return now, we may soon be out of hearing range.

Any accomplished human would be respected if they stopped their schedule and invited you into their lives. The same respect, and more, should be given to our accomplished God. The stars have no choice but to shine. Birds cannot refrain from singing. We, however, have the wonderful opportunity to obey God willingly. Let's us shine brightly and sing loudly the praises of our Accomplished King. Let us return.

Discussion question and Journal Space

1. Does the ability to return to God tempt you to sin, or draw you into intimacy, or both? What are the conditions when you draw close to God because of His grace?

_____

_____

_____

_____

_____

_____

_____

_____

_____

_____

CHAPTER TWENTY-ONE

Robbing God

Giving ten percent is far too easy.

Once while eating at a buffet with a group of friends I noticed one of my friends eating who hadn't paid for a plate. This bothered me greatly since God is clear in the Ten Commandments about not stealing. A sheriff walked in and I joked with my friend about reporting him. He wasn't amused, nor was he bothered in the least about his crime. For my own conscience's sake, I got back in line and bought him a plate.

His stealing seems justified to some. After all, what loss does a pizza joint really suffer if someone refuses to pay five bucks but still eats two or three slices of pizza? Stealing from   a higher, more powerful entity is often rationalized. Teachers take supplies home from school. Towels from hotels are packed into suitcases. What does it hurt? This pattern of stealing from the rich and powerful makes it even easier to collectively steal from God.

"Will a man rob God? Yet you have robbed Me! But you say, 'In what way have we robbed You?' In tithes and offerings. You are cursed with a curse, for you have robbed Me, even this whole nation. Bring all the tithes into the storehouse." - Malachi 3:8-10a

No one is wealthier or more powerful than God. He scoffs at attempts to buy His favor. He has no need of animal sacrifices since He owns the cattle on a thousand hills. He is not impressed with beautiful sanctuaries since the earth is His footstool. He would not come to man if He were hungry or thirsty. Scripture makes it clear; God lacks nothing.

Why would robbing such a God matter? We could never take anything away from God in a way that would decrease His wealth. All, but God, are zero sum. If you or I have twenty dollars and give three, we only have seventeen left. God has infinite resources, and after He generously shares, He still has infinite resources.

In one sense it is quite impossible to rob God. Today's moment with Malachi exposes the other side of the coin. There is a way to rob God, and God rebukes these thieves with passion.

Any and every time we fail to give God what He is due, we rob Him. We can rob Him by failing to give Him glory. We can rob Him by forgetting to thank Him. Many rob Him by refusing to surrender their talents and skills for use in His kingdom. Also, we rob Him by not giving financially the amount we ought. This is the robbery rebuked here in Malachi.

In the day of this rebuke, Jews were to give more than one tithe. Notice God doesn't tell them to start giving their tithe, but to give all the tithes. Ten percent was being given, but more than ten percent was required. Some biblical scholars say there were three tithes, a tithe that went to the Levites, a tithe that went toward feasts, and a tithe that helped those who were poor. All these tithes were not being offered, and God was being robbed because of it.

Very few believers today give three tithes. Very few give even ten percent, as a matter of fact. Does this mean God's rebuke could come to us as well? Are we robbing God?

Christians are not required to tithe, much to the regret of pastors who still tell them otherwise. Ten percent is not needed for Levites, nor is ten percent needed for feasts held in Jerusalem. Though there are many poor, there is no New Testament evidence that ten percent should be given to widows, orphans, and poor people either. The tithe, just as animal sacrifices, was eliminated when Christ offered Himself on our behalf upon the cross.

We are not required to tithe. However, God loves a cheerful giver and compliments those who give beyond their means. The tithe has been replaced by cheerful, sacrificial giving. Today we rob God if we give in any other way or if we refuse to give at all.

Giving ten percent is far too easy. There's no prayer involved; there's no passion needed; simply move the decimal point, and you're done. This kind of giving robs God. God wants us to include Him in our giving. He expects us to give cheerfully. He challenges us to give beyond our means. If we give sourly or sparingly, we rob God.

What do we take from God when we refuse to give? Is it money He wants? No, we rob God from revealing Himself to us. We rob God from transforming us. After all, where our treasure is, there our heart will be. We give money toward God's agenda so our heart will embrace God's agenda. When we fail to give, we rob ourselves more than anyone else. We lose, and God is sad. Wrestle with the question, am I robbing God? Then, for your own good, give.

Discussion Questions and Journal Space

1. Do you regularly give generously? If not, why not and when will you start?
2. When was a time you benefited from someone's generosity? Has there been a time when you were able to bless someone extravagantly by giving as unto the Lord?

_____

_____

_____

_____

_____

_____

_____

CHAPTER TWENTY-TWO

Testing God

"If I give cheerfully and sacrificially, will the rent be paid? What about the winter; it brings higher electric bills — and Christmas! How will I afford the winter if I give as I am convicted to give?"

Test God. If He fails you, then don't give the next time.

Of course, He won't fail you.

Only one place in scripture does God dare us to test Him. It's in Malachi, and during our moment, He'll encourage us to take the test. Testing God with our funds is a wonderful means of not robbing Him. We are instructed to give to such an extent that God's faithfulness is put to the test.

"'Bring all the tithes into the storehouse, that there may be food in My house, and try Me now in this,' says the LORD of hosts, 'If I will not open   for

*you the windows of heaven and pour out for you
such blessing that there will not be room enough
to receive it."* – Malachi 3:10

The original hearers of this promise were afraid of giving all tithes. They thought that giving so much might not allow them to eat all they wanted. They were concerned about saving enough for a bad harvest or a hard winter. God says to them clearly, "If you trust Me, I will pour out such a blessing it will be impossible for you to regret it."

We have the same promise. If we arrange our giving in such a way that tests God, we will not be embarrassed. Worries come quickly to us as well, however. "If I give cheerfully and sacrificially, will the rent be paid? What about the winter; it brings higher electric bills; and Christmas, how will I afford the winter if I give as I am convicted to give?" Test God. If He fails you, then don't give the next time around. Of course, He won't fail you.

Christians must test God by living more simply. Simplicity is a lifestyle that aims to give more than to gather. People who live simply enable themselves to invest much into the advancement of God's kingdom. People who do not live simply waste time and money building storage barns for their excess wealth. God dares us to give generously, and one of the ways we do this is by living simply. Living simply allows us to continue giving when God pours in blessings as well.

Your affections follow your funds, and your funds follow your affections. This offers a wonderful strategy. Test God with your giving, and you will find that as your money goes out, your affections go up. If you lack a heartfelt connection toward the needy, test God by giving much to the poor, and you'll soon have a deep, heartfelt connection toward the least.

Test God. Eat less and feed the hungry. Vacation less and take a mission trip. Have a family car instead of personal vehicles in order to pave the way for someone to go to college.

There are dozens of ways to test God. Equally, there are dozens of ways He will pour blessings back into your life.

This is not a financial gospel. The blessings may be far more valuable than paper money. Two fishermen discovered this one day. Peter and his brother, Andrew, had fished all night without catching anything. Jesus shows up at dawn and tells them to throw the net overboard one more time.

Jesus was saying, "Test Me." Of course Peter thought Jesus was nuts. Fishing is better at night, and in deeper water, plus the fishing was particularly poor on this day. Nevertheless, simply to test Jesus, Peter throws over the net. You know the rest of the story. The promise of Malachi came true. They caught so much fish they could not receive them all. They had to call their partners to help them pull in the nets.

What happens next is amazing. The text says, "And immediately they left everything and followed Him." Peter had just made the catch   of his life. The pay off would have been more than ever, but he leaves the fish to follow Jesus. The point of testing God with our time and money isn't to get more time and money, or fish. The point is to gain more of God.

You can have more of God. Test Him. Give in a way that puts His provision on the line. Take your Christmas money and give it away. Take your rent money and give it away. Doing so won't mean spending Christmas on the streets. Test God, then gain the best blessing, God Himself.

Plan to Obey

1. Test God with sacrificial giving of your money, your time, or both.

2. Tell someone, who has been used by God to bless your life, that you want to be used in a similar way. Tell them your plan, and ask them to pray for you. Use the next page to make notes about this process.

CHAPTER TWENTY-THREE

God does not pity the Christian

The best gift from God is God. All other gifts are simply to stimulate or allow us to embrace the primary gift of God Himself.

What an insult it would be to feel sorry for a Christian. With the greatest blessing, God Himself living inside them, they have everything they need. Having God means possessing the most valuable treasure. Pity should go to all those without God. Too often, as the Jews in Malachi's day, we walk as mourners complaining that the straight and narrow is too difficult a path.

"'Your words have been harsh against Me,' says the LORD, 'yet you say, 'What have we spoken against You?' You have said, 'It is useless to serve God; what profit is it that we have kept His ordinance, and that we have walked as mourners before the LORD of hosts? So now we call the proud blessed, for those who do wickedness are raised up; they even tempt God and go free.'" – Malachi 3:13-15

These Jews were totally task and religiously oriented. They thought mourning was a way of gaining pity from God. Why were they mourning? They mourned because they served God and didn't find immediate congratulations announced from the sky. To them, following God was bondage rather than freedom.

Many still fail to realize that the best gift from God is God. All other gifts are simply to stimulate or allow us to embrace the primary gift of God Himself. Forgiveness of sins, for example, is not an end, but a means. We are not supposed to love forgiveness for forgiveness's sake. If we do, we'll sin as often as possible to get it. We are supposed to enjoy forgiveness because it allows us to better enjoy God.

God must be treasured! Treasure, perhaps, should take precedence over Savior and Lord as titles for Christ. When He is viewed only as Savior, we are past oriented and may take much for granted. When He is viewed only as Lord, we are task oriented and may miss much grace. When He is Treasure, we love that He has saved us and we love to do His will.

God does not pity any Christian. To do so would dishonor His worth. God knows He is precious. He alone can be fully self-centered and fully God-centered at once. To be like God, we must declare His worth and pronounce Him precious. Any pity given for having God is a grave insult to a great King.

Not only did Malachi's Jews fail to treasure God, they failed to trust Him. They cried out that the proud were blessed and the humble neglected. They lost faith in God's ability to be just.

We must trust God. It is by faith that we are saved. We must trust that God is working everything together for His glory and our good. When it comes to the things of God, we should quickly and happily admit His ways are above our ways.

Trusting and treasuring is easy for children. Once I attended the Special Olympics and noticed this. In the Special Olympics there is always someone standing at the finish line cheering the runner. If there were no one there the athletes simply wouldn't run.

Running just to beat the other runners is a grown-up idea. If we desire to enter the kingdom of heaven, we'll run because Jesus stands at the finish line. Our running will be relational. Let's run in delight toward a Christ we treasure and trust.

Refuse to fall victim to dangerous comparison. These Jews had looked around and it seemed others were passing them in life's race. They were angry with God, but wouldn't have even noticed if they hadn't taken their eyes off Him.

We can trust God to make everything right one day. We can treasure Him in the meantime. One day the kids I saw running in the Special Olympics will run like the wind into the arms of Jesus who awaits their arrival. One day the weak and poor will be strong and rich. One day those who treasure anything but God will be disqualified and defeated. Let's run with childlike trust towards our Treasure. If you listen, you may hear Him cheering you on even now.

Discussion Questions and Journal Space

1. How can you fight the temptation to feel sorry for yourself?
2. Do you really believe that God will one day right every wrong and mend everything that's broken? In what ways can you live to show others you believe that?

CHAPTER TWENTY-FOUR

God wants to know what you said about Him

Fellowship is spiritual. When we read the Gospels, we find Christ often at people's houses eating their food. He spent much of His time talking. If the most holy Person who ever walked the face of the earth made a point to walk into peoples' homes and up to their tables, should we do any less?

God hears and sees all our activities. He listens, and He wants to know what we say about Him when we think He is unaware. None of our words are casual. All our words matter much because they imply how we feel about God. A moment with Malachi will reveal that   everyday conversation can be honored as passionate, tearful prayers.

"Then those who feared the LORD spoke to one another, and the LORD listened and heard them; so a book of remembrance was written before Him for those who fear the Lord and who meditate on His name. 'They shall be Mine,' says the LORD of hosts, on the day that I make them My jewels. I will spare them as a man spares his own son who serves him.' Then shall you again discern between the righteous and the wicked, between one who serves God and one who does not serve Him." – Malachi 3:16-18

God gives great attention to a group of people and plans to claim them as His children while others are judged. What do you think this group of people must have done to gain such an honor? Did they pray? Did they give? Did they evangelize? None of those activities are mentioned in this passage. Instead, God overheard people talking to each other about Him, liked what they said, and decided to act favorably towards them.

Many times church historians trace great revivals back to passionate sermons or concentrated prayer meetings. Both of these things are good, and no doubt do much to advance the kingdom of God. Wouldn't it be like God, however, to send a revival because He enjoyed a conversation He listened to during dinner?

What Malachi reports surprises, but it should also stimulate. Too often we gather for worship and then exit to our "real lives." If our preaching and prayers are not powerful enough to change our conversations, they may also fail at bringing revival. Could it be that God is waiting for a group of those who fear Him to get together and speak to one another?

God has given us a script, and we need to use it to discover our role and perfect our character. All we do is from Him and for Him. He listens in on every conversation and has ordained some of the words we say to be the cue for a wonderful, glorious plot twist.

God not only watches, He records. The giving and praying of Cornelius, for example, was mentioned in Acts 10:4, "Your prayers and alms have come up for a memorial before God." The salvation of every soul is written down in the Lamb's Book of Life. Tears are held in a bottle. It is not hard to believe God remembers prayers and giving and tears and conversions. It is not hard to believe these matter. Malachi reminds us, conversations matter too. God records our words and desires to hear us representing Him well in every conversation.

Nothing is casual. Everything matters because God matters. We must do all to the glory of God. Just as we gather for worship and prayer, just as we team up for evangelism and missions and service, we should realize a grand thing is happening when those that fear Him speak to one another.

Fellowship is spiritual. When we read the Gospels, we find Christ often at people's houses eating their food. He spent much of His time talking. If the most holy Person who ever walked the face of the earth made a point to walk into peoples' homes and up to their tables, should we do any less?

Many of the Jews in Malachi's day were skilled at putting on shows during temple time without allowing the presence of God to change their hearts. Christians today, unfortunately, have learned the same skill. Conversations reveal what is in the heart. Prayers can be faked, worship can be for show, but daily conversations are a good litmus test for faithfulness. When God listens let Him hear you sharing words that make your worship and prayers believable.

Journal Space: Be as aware as you can that God is listening to all you say about Him in the next twenty-four hours. Record some of the statements He overheard. What do you suppose His reaction is to all you said about Him?

_____

_____

_____

_____

_____

_____

_____

_____

_____

_____

_____

_____

CHAPTER TWENTY-FIVE

God must be crazy

He has enlisted us as soldiers. There will be a day when we are commanded to violently defeat those who oppose the Lord. This might be the truest test of our devotion.

One of the most amazing things about our God is that He shares. He doesn't just exist in the abstract. He shares His presence with us. He doesn't just hate our sin from a distance. He shares His conviction with us. He doesn't just tell us once from the sky how to live. He shares a book with us. From the beginning, He shared His image with us. At the climax of history, He shared His Son with us. Forever, He'll share His glory with us. He is a very generous God.

But there is a strange gift He wants to give you that you have probably never anticipated. God wants to share His wrath with you. I don't mean that He wants to share His wrath with you in the sense that you are the one getting His wrath. I mean that He wants you to share with you the experience of bringing wrath upon the wicked.

The first command of eternal celebration is not to begin eating at the Great Supper of the Lamb. It is not to begin singing songs of variety and pitch we could never imagine. The first command of eternal celebration is to participate in the punishing of the wicked. Once they are securely defeated and sentenced to eternal damnation, we will go about our eating, and drinking, and singing.

This isn't fantasy. Today's moment with Malachi teaches as much. We will participate in the judgment of God. Consider Malachi 4:1-3.

Surely the day is coming; it will burn like a furnace. All the arrogant and every evildoer will be stubble, and that day that is coming will set them on fire," says the LORD Almighty. "Not a root or a branch will be left to them. ² But for you who revere my name, the sun of righteousness will rise with healing in its wings. And you will go out and leap like calves released from the stall.

That's where we usually stop in our imagination. God will come down, consume the wicked with fire, gather up all the righteous, and we will forever be with the Lord. But look at the next verse.

Then you will trample down the wicked; they will be ashes under the soles of your feet on the day when I do these things," says the LORD Almighty.

God wants to share His judgment with us. We are not allowed to simply watch His war. He has enlisted us as soldiers. There will be a day when we are commanded to violently defeat those who oppose the Lord. This might be the truest test of our devotion.

In light of this, obvious and important questions surface within us. "Do I care about the honor of Jesus more than I care about the salvation of pagans? Do I care more about the honor of Jesus more than I care about the salvation of my friends? Do I care more about the honor of Jesus more than I care about the salvation of my family?"

All who claim to be Christians would say yes if asked, "Do you care about the honor of Jesus?" The question stretches us when we lay it beside other worthy cares. We quickly forget the honor of Jesus must be desired more than all other cares, even noble ones.

Spending a moment with Malachi today proves the Word of God can be a heavy load. The weight of God's Word often brings us to our knees. I believe that this moment with Malachi may be the heaviest of all. It must have been a message hard for Malachi to carry. It's certainly one hard for me to swallow.

God's generosity surpasses what we would dare to ever ask. He plans to include us in His holy execution of judgment. He will destroy the wicked with our help.

God's judgment is an intimate act of justice shared between Himself and His children. It is an intimate act because God draws close to us. It is shared because we witness His wrath and even are instruments of carrying out His wrath. How can this be? The God must be crazy!

All that honors Christ should also please us. God's wrath honors Christ because to forgive someone who rejected Him would insult the pain and agony of the cross. When the door of salvation opportunity closes, the people of God become the rain of God's next great flood.

What should our reaction be to this? Should we happily wait for our day of pouncing? No, we should join God in holy emotion that desires all to come to repentance. Still, we should join God in holy exaltation of Christ. Reach them now, so we do not trample them then.

Discussion Question and Journal Space

1. Many Christians no longer believe in hell.
   What's your position on God's eternal
   wrath? What scripture do you use to
   support this view?

_____

_____

_____

_____

_____

_____

_____

_____

_____

_____

CHAPTER TWENTY-SIX

The Sun of Righteousness Will Rise

If I can influence people who then influence others, I can gain crowns even after I die.

Malachi is not dead. He is part of the great cloud of witnesses watching us and talking to us as we run this Christian race. As you spent moments with Malachi, God added to his account because your heart has been changed.

The consequences of our lives are judged, not just our activities. This means if we want to bring God the maximum amount of glory and we want to bring ourselves the maximum amount of joy, we will live in a way that advances God's kingdom even after we die.

Consider if you rebuked someone for mistreating an employee. They receive your rebuke, and the employee keeps his or her job instead of quitting as they had planned. Soon, the employee gets a raise and uses some of that money to feed, clothe, and educate a child in a third- world country. Between you and this child stands the employee and the boss friend you rebuked, but you still get directly blessed for advancing the kingdom.

Our imagination could play further into what the child in the third-world is able to accomplish since food, clothing, and education has been provided. Upon entering heaven there may be many rewards you had no idea you had inherited.

My point is that your influence, not just your activity, gains you crowns in heaven, crowns that you will be able to throw at the feet of Jesus someday. Since I love Jesus, I want to be throwing crowns at his feet for as long as possible. There's no way I could gain all the crowns I want during my life from my activity. But if I can influence people who then influence others, I can gain crowns even after I die.

I am motivated to follow Malachi's guidance not just for God's glory, but also for Malachi's joy. This guy deserves credit for carrying his burden and delivering his daring words. When you and I obey, we increase the amount of crowns he gets to throw.

Malachi four has the most beautiful image of God; the image of the sun rising in the east. A sun that makes everything right that was wrong will soon rise, and in that moment we will all be captivated. In that moment surprising rewards will rain down around us. We will meet those who influenced our lives without our knowledge. We will take up our crowns together and throw them at the feet of our shared Savior.

Very soon all will be swallowed up with either the presence of God or the absence of God. All will be greeted with either the smile of God or the frown of God. All will be given an eternal sentence, either, "well done," or "depart from Me." Eternal joy or eternal torment is the destination of every person on the globe. Both groups are described in Malachi 4:1-3.

"'For behold, the day is coming, burning like a furnace; and all the arrogant and every evildoer will be chaff; and the day that is coming will set them ablaze,' says the LORD of hosts, "so that it will leave them neither root nor branch. But for you who fear My name, the sun of righteousness will rise with healing in its wings; and you will go forth and skip about like calves from the stall. You will tread down the wicked, for they will be ashes under the soles of your feet on the day which I am preparing,' says the LORD of hosts."

Yesterday we concentrated on the judgment of the wicked. Today we will focus on the redemption of the righteous. For those who fear God's name, the sun of righteousness will rise with healing in His wings. Let's take a moment with Malachi to meditate on the healings that will come to us that day, and realize that much of it can come to us now.

The sun brings heat where there is coldness. This is a needed healing today. We must admit, our emotions toward Christ are too cold. We don't feel like intimately connecting with Him through regular worship or scripture reading or prayer. We make attempts to live within intellectual Christianity only. When the sun of righteousness rises with healing, lukewarm worship will heat into eternal white-hot flames.

The sun brings growth where there is barrenness. Will you admit that you are not producing the fruit you should as a Christian? Do you have a healthy diet of Christian disciplines? Do you feed your soul with television more than Scripture? Do you desire to gain more than you desire to distribute? Aren't there seeds of potential in you lying dormant because you aren't watering them or exposing them to the sun of righteousness?

The sun brings light where there is darkness. There are things misunderstood that will be totally clear on that day. Darkness covers so much of God. Much of His activity is hidden. Many of His reasons are unseen. The people of God see only vaguely what's going on and must live by faith that all will be well. But on the day the sun of righteousness rises with healing, there will be no darkness. Insights will pour into our brain and worship will pour out of our hearts as we enter a time where shadows cease, and God is face to face.

Discussion Questions and Journal Space

1. What healing or recovery do you most look forward to at Jesus' return?
2. How would your life change if you admit that the consequences of your life will be judged, not just the limited activities of it?

_____

_____

_____

_____

CHAPTER TWENTY-SEVEN

Our God has wings

There is far too much evil in the world
today, but soon this will change.

The healing that awaits all who follow Christ
comes from a winged God. Presently, we are safe
beneath the shadow of His wings, but soon we
will be set free from all shadows. Every curse
will transform into blessing. God will open His
wings, and we will take flight.

There is far too much evil in the world
today. There is a curse that taints all human
experience. Honesty is taken as insult. Love
turns too easily to lust. Boldness appears to be
arrogance. The curse is a poison, handicapping
all who wish to walk with Christ. There is far too

much evil in the world today, but soon this will change.

The sun of righteousness will rise with healing in His wings, and all those who are handicapped will become healthy. There will be a great march back into the garden. The lame will run; the blind will see; the deaf will hear. All will smell and taste the glory and grace of God's only Son. The great curse will be crippled.

There will be a second creation of sorts. Physical disabilities will cease. Mental slowness will speed to new intelligence. Those relationally scared and scarred will have confidence to completely trust the nations surrounding the throne.

Best of all, healing will replace sin. Our sinful flesh will fall off and new bodies will be given. The taint will turn to splendor. There will be no more tears.

These are the healings we await. Christ, the sun of righteousness, brings these healings. There's no reason to guess how you'll react   that day; Malachi wrote it down. Verse two says you will skip or leap like a calf from the stall.

Please use your imagination to see an enormous titan with wings bent over a calf, keeping it in the shadow of its wings. The titan must do this because there are great predators that would kill the calf if it were exposed. But the day is coming when the titan will spread its wings and knock down all those predators. They will be totally destroyed and then the calf will jump for joy in green pastures.

This is our reality. God protects us now. We live in the stall of His protection. We are in His hands so to speak. On the day the sun of righteousness rises with healing, we will be set down to run freely. But we'll do more than just run – we will leap and skip! Our bodies will be able to do what our heart has done.

Surely your heart has leaped within you. On your marriage day, when your kids were born, during a great film – your heart has jumped in your chest. At the end of semester exams, as you stood at the base of a mountain, or witnessed a shooting star – your heart has leaped within you. These are just foreshadowing of the real leaping to come.

On this day our whole bodies will leap. We will leap like a calf leaving the stall. We will leap for joy. We will leap for freedom. We will leap because we'll finally be healed. That's our destination, and our destination should make a difference.

Journal a prayer thanking God for the restoration He will bring to this earth. List all you'll be happy to see fixed.

_____

_____

_____

_____

_____

_____

CHAPTER TWENTY-EIGHT

How should we respond?

Remember the Law of Moses, My servant, which I commanded him in Horeb for all Israel, with the statutes and judgments. Behold, I will send Elijah the prophet before the coming of the great and dreadful day of the LORD. And he will turn the hearts of the fathers to the children, and the hearts of the children to their fathers, lest I come and strike the earth with a curse.

– Malachi 4:4-6

At the end of a long walk, how do you say goodbye to a friend? Malachi has been faithful to tell the truth in love. God has been faithful to strengthen your soul as you spent moments with Malachi. How should you respond? There is no need to guess. Malachi gives specific instructions at the end of his text.

The last words of Malachi are important. We are threatened with a curse if we do not obey them. To finish strong we are to look back at the Word of God, look forward to the coming of God, and look around at the people of God. Unless we look where Malachi points, we will become stiff-necked people.

Over and over again, and everyday, we must look back into the Word of God. The Bible is the primary source of Christian faith. We must be people of this book. If we hide the Word in our hearts, we will not sin against Him. If we meditate on the Word, and make it our delight we will be like trees planted beside steams of living water.

Of course, we are not just to read the Bible. We are to remember the Law of Moses. We are to consider what the words say. We must ask, "What difference does that make for me?" We don't just read, "I can do all things through Christ who strengthens me." We ask, "What difference does that make for me." When we really consider, and then remember the words of scripture, they make a huge difference indeed.

Nothing will direct our lives like the Bible. The words of others can encourage and instruct, but they fail to bring our souls to life like scripture. Even the Holy Spirit will never say anything to us that scripture doesn't support. Reading the Bible helps us learn the difference between the voice of Satan, our own imagination, and God's Holy Spirit. Each time Jesus was tempted, He resisted with, "for it is written." We cannot do better than Christ; we must look back into the book!

Malachi instructs us also to look forward. The great and dreadful day of the Lord is coming, we are told. The Day of Judgment will be dreadful to all who don't know Him, and great for all who do. We should anticipate this day with hope and delight. We should pray for faith to stand before the Son of Man.

Our entire lives must be bent on the hope that Christ is returning. If this future event is false, our lives should look utterly ridiculous. Above all others, we should be pitied if there is no resurrection. Our prayers should look silly if there is no resurrection. Our giving should be ludicrous without a place without rust where thieves do not break in and steal.

The Jews were to anticipate John and their Messiah. We are to anticipate Christ's return. There should be times when we get homesick looking to the eastern sky. Our rote prayer should turn to tears at times when we pray, "Your kingdom come." We look forward toward our home and glorious Treasure.

Finally, Malachi instructs us to look around at each other. Fathers should look toward their children. Friends should look toward each other. This journey of salvation is one that is shared. Two are better than one, and a group of three is stronger still.

What a difference it would make to take these last instructions seriously. Curses are lifted as we look into God's word, look forward to His return, and look around with compassion for others. The curse spreads like a plague when we refuse.

I love the book of Malachi. He begins with love for God, and ends with love for neighbor. The parts in between simply elaborate on these two great commands. We must love God by giving pure offerings and remembering our covenant. We must love neighbors by staying pure in every relationship and respecting our community. Malachi acts as a gate into the straight and narrow. Now, let us begin to walk it faithfully.

Thanks for purchasing and reading *Moments with Malachi!* Let's stay connected!

I would love to hear how God spoke to you as you read this book. I can be reached at www.upandoutpublishing.com.

This book isn't meant to be read alone. It best serves as a teaching tool for groups or a shared read between accountability partners. Please consider using the book this way. Copies can be purchased in bulk at a discounted rate. To learn more, contact me at prowritermike@gmail.

Finally, I would love to be able to meet you and speak to your group! If you are a teacher and you used *Moments with Malachi* as a teaching resource, please let me know about it, and I'll try to come meet your group and thank you personally.

Many blessings and thanks!
Michael Powell

Made in the USA
Coppell, TX
30 November 2020